"This luminous book delivers a synthe [...] both *personal* and *profound*, arising fro [...] *Sent Forth* radiates with the new ardo [...] sions called for by the New Evangelization, drawing upon recent popes and St. John Henry Newman as guardians and guides. Anyone seeking to enkindle in themselves the fire of the Church's mission to proclaim the gospel should read this book."

—**Matthew Kuhner**, vice president and academic dean, St. Bernard's School of Theology and Ministry

"The Saint John Society is one of the bright spots in a time of crisis in the world and in the Church. I am grateful that members of the Society have put into writing the 'secrets' that have made their life and mission so fruitful. All those interested in moving forward in confidence in response to the call for a new evangelization will find this book of great help."

—**Ralph Martin**, author of *The Fulfillment of All Desire*

"I have for a long time come to believe that the Church must return to her roots, recapture her deepest identity, and recommit herself to the essential mission entrusted to her by the bridegroom, Jesus Christ our Lord. That mission is to proclaim the gospel of Jesus Christ to the people of our time, especially in the secularized world in which we live. I am confident that *Sent Forth* will be an effective and practical resource in that great mission."

—**Alexander Sample**, archbishop of Portland, Oregon

"*Sent Forth* provides an inspirational and in-depth description of what it means to be on mission today. Focusing on proclamation, the kerygma, and the process of conversion, the authors also illuminate the centrality of prayer, spiritual power, and personal influence in the work of evangelization. For those seeking to do mission today—to fulfill the commission to make disciples of all nations—this book is a treasure chest of wisdom and insight."

—**Dan Keating**, author of *The Adventure of Discipleship*

"This slender volume, as its title indicates, is a handbook mirroring one way of living the mission of the Lord Jesus in the world today. The subject of this book, then, is the missionary method of the Saint John Society. A breath of the fervor of the early church and of the Acts of the Apostles generously blows throughout this text. The freshness and vigor of its atmosphere clearly derives from the hands-on practice of the apostolate rather than from theory."

—**Simeon Leiva-Merikakis**, OCSO, author of *Fire of Mercy, Heart of the Word*

Sent Forth

Sent Forth

Handbook for a Missionary Church

Fr. Ignacio Llorente, and
Michael Ceragioli

Foreword by
Simeon Leiva-Merikakis

 CASCADE *Books* · Eugene, Oregon

SENT FORTH
Handbook for a Missionary Church

Cascade Books
An Imprint of Wipf and Stock Publishers
199 W. 8th Ave., Suite 3
Eugene, OR 97401

www.wipfandstock.com

PAPERBACK ISBN: 978-1-6667-6489-5
HARDCOVER ISBN: 978-1-6667-6490-1
EBOOK ISBN: 978-1-6667-6491-8

Cataloguing-in-Publication data:

Names: Llorente, Ignacio, author. | Ceragioli, Michael, author. | Leiva-Merikakis,
Simeon, foreword.

Title: Sent Forth : handbook for a Missionary Church / by Ignacio Llorente and
Michael Ceragioli ; foreword by Simeon Leiva-Merikakis.

Description: Eugene, OR : Cascade Books, 2023. | Includes bibliographical refer-
ences.

Identifiers: ISBN 978-1-6667-6489-5 (paperback) | ISBN 978-1-6667-6490-1 (hard-
cover) | ISBN 978-1-6667-6491-8 (ebook)

Subjects: LCSH: Catholic Church—Missions—United States. | Missions—Theory.

Classification: BV219 .L65 2023 (print) | BV219 .L65 (ebook)

03/16/23

Scripture texts used in this work are taken from the New American Bible, revised edition * 2010, 1991, 1986, 1970 Confraternity of Christian Doctrine Inc., Washington
DC. All rights reserved.

The authors gratefully acknowledge permission from Sherry Weddell to use a graphic
inspired by her book *Forming Intentional Disciples: The Path to Knowing and Following
Jesus* (Huntington, IN: Our Sunday Visitor, 2012).

Contents

Foreword

THIS SLENDER VOLUME, AS its title indicates, is a handbook mirroring one way of living the mission of the Lord Jesus in the world today. But don't let the modest term 'handbook' deceive you into thinking that what it offers is merely a dry set of principles and abstract guidelines on how best to steer the missionary task of the Catholic Church in our present society. What I admire above all in this engaging little work is its enthusiasm for the mission already undertaken by the Saint John Society, and its members' deep sense of personal vocation to their mission, rooted in the centrality of the Lord Jesus in a life of communion with him through ardent prayer, both individual and fraternal.

The subject of this book, then, is the missionary method of the Saint John Society, a 'society of apostolic life' founded some 20 years ago in Argentina and now with ministries also in the United States, Italy, and Uruguay. This handbook offers the fruits of a joint effort between a priest of the Society and a layman who closely collaborates with the Society's mission.

A breath of the fervor of the early Church and of the Acts of the Apostles generously blows throughout this text. The freshness and vigor of its atmosphere clearly derives from the hands-on practice of the apostolate rather than from theory, although the fruits of solid Catholic doctrine and its assiduous study may be detected everywhere.

The main title of the book, *Sent Forth*, is of solid biblical resonance. It evokes not only the lives of this Society's *Apostles*, 'those sent forth', but above all points to the *Sender* who initiates the process and stresses the specific *Mission* he intends. Insofar as any life experience can be distilled in words, this book represents the heart of the life the apostles of the Saint John Society are living with admirable vibrancy. As such, the text is itself a missionary endeavor, an attempt by the members of the Society to communicate the Word they have personally received, as well as the reason for their fraternal joy, shared convictions and central driving-force.

To me, the authenticity of their apostolate is demonstrated by the fact that the only reward they expect for their labors is the love of the Lord whom they strive to serve as brothers united in faith and hope. They realize that true love can be repaid only by more love, hence the motto of the Society, borrowed from Saint John Henry Newman, its theologian and patron of choice: *Cor ad cor loquitur*—'Heart speaks to heart'. The motto connotes a sought-for depth of communication that calls for both divine and human communion and that creates unbreakable bonds of charity.

This handbook draws on influential resources like Newman and describes the actual practice of the missionary life, particularly among young people and the needy of society. However, the heart of the endeavor of the members of the Saint John Society, and thus the compelling focus of their attention, is the love Jesus Christ and the responsibility they owe him for having accepted his call to their apostolate. The strongest element of the book, therefore, is its rootedness in the life of fervent prayer, leading day-to-day to ever greater intimacy with the Lord Jesus. Such prayer is, in turn, founded objectively on the frquent practice of *lectio divina*, which is the apostles' daily bread and guarantees they will not, through busyness or human weakness, lose sight of the living Person whose love has claimed their hearts irreversibly.

The Scripture reference that the Saint John Society has chosen as the bedrock for its vocation is the account of Jesus' calling of the Twelve in the Gospel of Mark: "And he went up on the mountain and called to him those whom he desired, and they came to him. And he made twelve (whom he also named apostles) so that they might be with him and he might send them out to preach" (Mk 3:13-14). Here we see clearly the wise hierarchy of Jesus' intentions. The primary and supreme purpose why Jesus calls to himself his intended apostles is *that they might be with him,* which is to say that they might enter into a particularly intimate association with himself, that they might share his life continually in all its aspects, and thus become close friends of his Heart.

Only then, in second place, and as a result of that intimate sharing of Jesus' life, those first *called to himself* by Jesus are then *sent forth* by him from his presence, to proclaim the Good News and bring many others to a similarly familiar relationship with the Savior.

'Salvation', in this perspective, is nothing other than a life of sustained, vibrant union with Christ. As such, salvation cannot be a human work, impelled solely by human initiative and desire. Rather, salvation is a work of God carried out by grace through the collaboration of human beings who are themselves the first in need of redemption. The work of the priest-apostle of the Saint John Society, like that of every Christian apostle, is to open up the gates of salvation to a hungry and yearning world. Yet, for it to have divine vigor and urgency, such a work must always be seen as secondary to, and wholly deriving from, the apostle's foremost occupation: namely, his intimate relationship with Jesus, which he must carefully and untiringly cultivate, day and night.

Evangelization, if it is to be genuine, can never be its own end, the result of a well-intentioned humanitarian project. Fruitful evangelization, the kind that communicates the living and life-giving Word of God, can only be the *byproduct* of a life lived in intimacy with Christ, with the apostle drawing deeply from the "wells of salvation" (Is 12:3), both for himself and for all those he sets out to evangelize. On this uncompromising truth the Saint John Society has staked its every effort and its very identity, preferring nothing to the love of Christ—not even the apparent success of the mission.

Simeon Leiva-Merikakis, OCSO

St Joseph's Abbey, Spencer

Introduction

IN OUR MINISTRIES IN the Saint John Society, we find ourselves returning to Jesus's Great Commission as the source of our inspiration. As Jesus sent his disciples forth to the ends of the earth, so too do we find his sending to be the imperative of our work today: we have been sent forth to preach the gospel so as to send others out in turn. Founded in Argentina in 2001, the Saint John Society is an apostolic community inspired by the public life of Jesus, dedicated to the New Evangelization. It has grown to establish centers of evangelization in Italy, Uruguay, and the United States. We write presently, one priest and one lay person, as witnesses to the action of Christ in parishes that have sprung to life, in the hearts of college and high school students, in the urban and rural poor, and in whole immigrant families and communities that have come to faith. We write as grateful participants in the generative pattern of growth in Christ that we have seen not only in our ministries but throughout the Church: that is, transformative encounter with the Holy Spirit, leading to a newfound commitment to Christ, on to earnest participation within a faith community, and back out to share with the world.

This is not *our* secret but the *open secret* of New Life in Christ! We begin from the conviction that the Holy Spirit is presently inviting the Church to move forward into the fullness of her identity as a truly missionary Church. *The Church exists to evangelize!* You are called to be a part of this missionary endeavor, wherever you might estimate you stand today. As a Church, our primary task is to announce Christ and the New Life he brings to those who do not know him, and our primary means is the power of the Holy Spirit. We believe Christ wants to outdo the wave of unbelief— to counteract the seductions of untrammeled secularism—through a new anointing of his Holy Spirit. He is making all things new. He will accomplish what he started. With an ear pressed to his heart, we move forward with a spirit of victory founded upon the resurrection of Christ. We stand upon faith upheld in hope but also upon our delight that this renewal is already happening in our midst. We speak not just as isolated individuals called to a special task but as members of a people sent forth!

This book seeks to serve as an encouragement and a tool for all those endeavoring to live out Christ's universal call to mission. It is a resource for those who want to find their footing in the river of life to which the saints are constantly making their appeal. We write as missionaries of the New Evangelization who wish to provide theological and practical support as you travel along your personal path of discipleship. In what follows, we aim not only to share experiences from our ministries but also to highlight the work of current and past theologians, recent popes, and lay evangelists who have shaped our vision of evangelization.

We begin by examining the Great Commission and the phenomenon of conversion. As it has always been, the main task of the Church today is to make disciples. We are called to lead others to faith by announcing the message of Jesus, called to give ourselves over to a mysterious process composed of a confluence of diverse and complementary factors. We will look at the content of the message of the good news on the one hand (the scriptural foundations of the process) and, on the other, the stages that people pass through on their way to faith (the process itself).

We approach our topic through what we have dubbed the Five Ps of Evangelization, the core factors that lead people to faith. The evangelizer needs to be acquainted with the following central concepts:

1. **Proclamation:** The kerygma (kə-ˈrig-mə), or the preaching of the good news. We touch on the transmission of the truth of Christianity through teaching and reading, and we outline the fundamental tenets of the Christian worldview.

b. **Personal Influence:** The Christian life must be modeled to be properly understood. The personal influence of a Christian who embodies Jesus's sayings about becoming the salt and light of the earth accomplishes what mere catechesis cannot.

c. **Persuasion:** The attractiveness of goodness, truth, and beauty; how these transcendental pathways to Christ impact seekers.

d. **Prayer:** Intercession influences the heart from within, going out ahead of mission. We discuss the necessity of personal holiness in the active life. Prayer is the sine qua non of mission.

e. **Power:** The power of the Holy Spirit as exercised through signs and wonders. We live in an age skeptical of all that might be deemed "miraculous." Yet, many among us testify to personal transformation through supernatural intervention, either through healings or messages from on high. What is the place of signs and wonders in the work of evangelization? When do denial of signs and wonders constitute a lack of trust, and when does reliance on signs and wonders pull us away from right priorities?

Saint John Henry Newman, intellectual father of the Saint John Society and important protagonist of this book, provides a striking example of response to the Great Commission, as he invites the Church to announce the gospel in all circumstances. In his "Twelfth Discourse to Mixed Congregations," he delivers this spirited assessment to the Christians before him:

> It is no new thing with the Church, in a time of confusion or of anxiety, when offenses abound, and the enemy is at her gates, that her children, far from being dismayed, or rather glorying in the danger, as vigorous men exult in trials of their strength—it is no new thing, I say, that they should go forth to do her work, as though she were in the most palmy days of her prosperity. Old Rome, in her greatest distress, sent her legions to foreign destinations by one gate, while the Carthaginian conqueror was at the other. In truth, as has been said of our own countrymen, we, Catholics, do not know when we are beaten; we advance, when by all the rules of war we ought to fall back; we dream but of triumphs, and mistake (as the world judges) defeat for victory. For we have upon us the omens of success in the recollections of the past; we read upon our banners the names of many an old field of battle and of glory; we are strong in the strength of our fathers, and we mean to do, in our humble measure, what saints have done before us.[1]

Ultimately, Newman came to be numbered among these servants of God whom he acclaimed. He did not allow the perplexities and mixed messages present in the Church of his times to prevent him from embracing his mission of renewal. He strode out on the principle that the record of faithful Christians and the personal longing for a better future point in the same direction: forward. May we be like him. May we keep advancing, whatever we surmise the forecast to be. May we go forth—precisely as those *sent forth* in love!

---

1. DMC, "Discourse 12," 243–44.

Abbreviations

AP   Newman, John Henry. "Lecture 7: Assumed Principles the Intellectual Ground of the Protestant View." From *Present Position of Catholics in England*. Newman Reader, 2007. https://www.newmanreader.org/works/england/lecture7.html.

APVS   Newman, John Henry. *Apologia pro Vita Sua*. New York: Penguin, 1995.

CCC   *Catechism of the Catholic Church*. 2nd ed. Washington, DC: United States Conference of Catholic Bishops, 2019.

CT   John Paul II. *Catechesi Tradendae (On Catechesis in Our Time)*. Manchester, NH: Sophia Institute, 2014.

DMC   Newman, John Henry. *Discourses Addressed to Mixed Congregations*. London: Longmans, Green, and Co., 1902.

EG   Francis. *The Joy of the Gospel (Evangelii Gaudium)*. Boston: Pauline, 2013.

EM   Newman, John Henry. *Two Essays on Biblical and on Ecclesiastical Miracles*. Works of Cardinal Newman: Birmingham Oratory Millennium Edition. Notre Dame, IN: Notre Dame University Press, 2010.

EN   Paul VI. *On Evangelization in the Modern World (Evangelii Nuntiandi)*. Boston: Pauline, 1976.

LG   *Lumen Gentium*. In *Vatican II: The Conciliar and Postconciliar Documents*, edited by Austin Flannery, OP, 350–426. Collegeville, MN: Liturgical, 1996.

MD   Newman, John Henry. *Meditations and Devotions*. Mahwah, NJ: Paulist, 2010.

PG   Patrologia Graeca. Edited by J.-P. Migne. 162 vols. Paris, 1857–1886.

PI   Newman, John Henry. "Sermon 5: Personal Influence, the Means of Propagating the Truth." From *Oxford University Sermons*. Newman Reader, 2007. https://www.newmanreader.org/works/oxford/sermon5.html.

PPS   Newman, John Henry. *Parochial and Plain Sermons*. Vol. 4. London: Longmans, Green & Co, 1909.

RM   John Paul II. *Mission of the Redeemer (Redemptoris Missio)*. Boston: Pauline, 1991.

WR   Newman, John Henry. "Witness to the Resurrection." In *Parochial and Plain Sermons*, 1:181–88. San Francisco: Ignatius, 1997.

CHAPTER ONE

The Great Commission: Christ, Contemporary to Us

LIVING IN THE STATE of Oregon, you become spoiled by a variety of beautiful landscapes: the high partition of the Cascade Mountain Range locks in the moisture coming off the ocean in the far western portion of the state and thus keeps the territory marvelously green, while accustoming the east to generous sunshine. The mountains and waterways carve out a unique set of destinations: starting from Portland, you have the Willamette River bisecting the city, the beaches a drive away in the west, a stretch of high-elevation desert within reach to the east, and dense forests sheltering lakes on both sides of the mountain divide. Yet if you ask a native Oregonian, outstanding even among the beauties of the Northwest are the headwaters of the Metolius River, located on the eastern side of the Cascades next to Black Butte Mountain. According to many scientists, the Metolius flows from a hidden spring inside the mountain. Having been told about the headwaters often enough, we took a trip out with a group from our parish—not to the interior of the mountain, of course, but to where we could see the river in the light of day. We aimed to get as close to the source as we could, stopping right where the maps indicated that the headwaters broke out into the open. And how disappointed we were! Anticipating a cascading, pure torrent of water, we instead found a feeble stream, practically whimpering as it emerged into the sunshine.

When we drove away from the source, downriver for about ten miles, we at last found ourselves next to the awe-inspiring mighty current we had initially envisioned. What started small had gathered force, drawing on neighboring creeks and mountain streams to become a most impressive river. The Metolius presents a good metaphor for the nature and development of Catholic Christianity. At the heart of Christianity, we have both a hidden wellspring and a stream that ongoingly flows from that wellspring. The hidden wellspring is the person of Christ from whom the fullness of life flows into his body—into us, that is. Behind everything we see in the Church lies the resurrection of Christ, the hidden source—hidden in the first place because none but the Father and the Holy Spirit are privy to the event of Jesus rising from the dead and emerging from his tomb; and hidden in the second place because his presence in every age can be accessed only through faith.

Although his presence may be hidden, it remains real, powerful, and *flowing*. In John 7, Jesus says that "rivers of living water" will flow from those who believe in him (John 7:38), indicating the fruit of his resurrection and the coming of the Holy Spirit. The hidden wellspring of the Church is the glorious and resurrected body of Jesus, and the living water that flows from him is the Holy Spirit. Jesus's resurrection stands at the origin of a stream of life that runs throughout history.

Like the Metolius, this stream of life began small. If judging by the appearance of initial strength alone, if judging as it were by sight from an early overlook point, who would predict the transformation of the world through this Jesus and the followers loyal to him? Jesus appeared to only a few selected witnesses. These witnesses were bereft of the web of connections, resources, and farseeing tactics that historians present as the essential material for the instigation of the movement of the ages. But those who encountered the risen Christ were filled with the life of their teacher and in turn shared the New Life they received with others; more by way of obedience than foresight, they tapped into a means of transmission and development that proved to possess a world-transforming power all its own. In due time, the initial stream carved out its course inexorably, defying obstacles and gathering force as it traveled throughout nations and across ages.

We testify to this current of life—that we have been reached, awed, and filled; and that we are accordingly impelled to share. This book, above all else, aims to transmit the central conviction that Jesus is alive, and that he wants to share his New Life, the life of the Holy Spirit, with the world today. "The Church exists to evangelize," wrote Pope Paul VI; the Church exists to share the life of her Lord without inhibition.[1] To put the matter baldly: the Church exists for the purpose of immersing people into that river of New Life so that they may experience the joy that transforms hearts—and

---

1. EN, para. 14.

so that from their place, they may in turn transform others. The Church is not to be an enclosed group that exists only for the purposes of her current members but a perpetually outward-facing community oriented towards helping all people towards a relationship with Jesus.

Let's start our investigation into this task by engaging in a *lectio divina* (divine reading) of the version of the Great Commission found in the Gospel of Matthew. The Great Commission sets the tone and establishes the framework to understand the missionary imperative explored in the upcoming chapters of this book. We will reflect on Jesus's command to go forth, as well as three key actions of the Church: to make disciples, to baptize, and to teach. In *lectio divina* style, read the text through closely before proceeding:

> All power in heaven and on earth has been given to me. Go, therefore, and make disciples of all nations, baptizing them in the name of the Father, and of the Son, and of the holy Spirit, teaching them to observe all that I have commanded you. And behold, I am with you always, until the end of the age. (Matt 28:18–20)

Go: The Heart of Mission

In the television drama *The Chosen*, which imaginatively retells the life of Jesus, the Pharisee Nicodemus meets Mary Magdalene a little while after Jesus has forgiven, delivered, and healed her. Remembering well her pitiable former condition, Nicodemus is intensely curious about the circumstances of her healing; he cannot help himself as he unloads a barrage of questions. Mary has at last had enough of the interrogation. Cutting him off, she says: "Here is what I know. I was one way, and now I am completely different. The thing that happened in between was him."[2] Mary's response might stand as the succinct account of the transformation that Christ brings to our lives. As we reflect upon the first imperative of the Great Commission—"go"—we should begin with the foundational (and always concrete) experience that drives mission. What is at the heart of our mission? Like Mary Magdalene, we were one way—patterned according to guilt, sin, sadness, pessimism—but Jesus came, and now we are different.

Fulton Sheen used to say that the gospel starts with the word "come" and ends with the word "go." His observation has an existential validity:

---

2. Jenkins, *Chosen*, 24:00.

people first come to Christ, experience New Life, and then go out to share it with others. It is almost a law of action found in the New Testament: people touched by Jesus go to tell others. They surprise no one as much as themselves. They go out unmistakably belonging to Jesus. They go out with something to do, something that shatters their own expectations of life and their previous idea of who they were. Not only baptism but Jesus's call, too, proves to be a form of rebirth. Like the Magi who return to their country by another way (Matt 2:12), the going implies a direction of life different from what prevailed in the coming.

Consider this brief catalog from the New Testament: Mary receives the annunciation from the angel Gabriel and sets off in haste to visit Elizabeth (Luke 1:39). The shepherds experience the reality of heaven and travel to Bethlehem (Luke 2:15). Matthew is called from the tax collector's table and immediately invites his friends to a party with Jesus (Matt 9:10). The man delivered from demons returns to his home and announces what Jesus has done for him (Mark 5:19). The Samaritan woman, trailed by broken relationships and living in open scandal, drinks of the living water and tells the whole town about the Messiah (John 4:39). The women at the tomb hear the message of resurrection from the angels and run to the apostles (Luke 24:9). Mary Magdalene encounters the Risen Jesus and becomes the apostle to the apostles (John 20:18). Paul encounters the Risen Jesus along the road and begins to proclaim him (Acts 9).

Jesus's first command of the Great Commission begins with the simple declarative: "Go!" But this beginning is not exactly a proper start, as it takes the whole rest of the saving work of Jesus in view; the imperative "go" is preceded—necessarily so—by the experience of New Life, the coming. The mission of the Church started with a community of witnesses who experienced the New Life in Christ. Looking back to the veritable headwaters of the Metolius, we find these initial witnesses who discovered the hidden source and started to receive the New Life that flows from the resurrected body of Jesus. They embody the primordial, irreplaceable experience of evangelization: to believe in the transforming power of Jesus!

The Pattern Observed Today

If "come" is the opening invitation of the great story of New Life and "go" the closing summons, then the power of grace is the driving energy, the in-between that ties the cord between Christ's beckoning and his sending. It is the grace of God that anticipates and leads towards any change made by an individual; grace is the "vertical factor"—that which interrupts the self-told tale of the unwitting one who is on the way to becoming a witness; grace enters and opens the path for a life built around the gift of New Life. Grace provides the motivation to grow, the at first shrouded but then increasingly within reach certainty that personal change is possible, and that this change is marked by deepening conformity to the heart of Jesus.

Everything begins with this stirring of grace, which animates the spiritual life. In Catholic life, it is not enough just to repeat devotions; our faith is about experiencing life in Christ through the power of the Holy Spirit. This experience of New Life is the experience of Saint Paul, of Mary Magdalene, of the tax collectors, of the fishermen, and of all the healed men and women, named and unnamed, of the New Testament. The same Spirit that gave life to them transforms us today, as the impulse to share takes root. In our work of evangelization, we have seen this pattern at work so many times and arising through such unforeseeable circumstances that we continue to be amazed. The creativity of God knows no bounds. This vision of renewal in Christ is the great privilege of mission: in a certain way, the Gospels and the Acts of the Apostles are reenacted today, as we get a taste of the profound healings and conversions written of in Jesus's ministry and in the ministry of his disciples.

We could tell countless amazing stories of people who have experienced New Life in Christ and in turn began to share it with others, but we want to offer just one exemplary testimony to illustrate this principle at work. We met a woman in her mid-twenties through a retreat in eastern Oregon. Three months after the event, she wrote a letter revealing that coming into the weekend, she had been planning to end her life the week after the retreat. She had struggled with depression for years, and she had already attempted suicide several times. She had recently been hospitalized after a mental health crisis. She went to the retreat thinking it would be the last spiritual event of her life, that she would take it as an opportunity to make a good confession before leaving this earth behind. Here is a portion of her testimony:

> I was not planning for anything profound to happen on the retreat. I didn't want to be vulnerable with others. Even though I had definitive plans to end my life, I believe God was already calling me back to him. On Saturday, I sensed that something—something stored up within me and previously untouchable—was unraveling.

We had confession, which began to open my heart. We had our activities. We were having fun. Then we returned to the center for our holy hour. I had never done adoration before in my life. When I went into the chapel, I could feel I was starting to cry. I have always been a crybaby. I was trying to hold it in because I didn't want people to hear me sniffling. I asked God to enter into my heart. After that, I began to choke on my sobs. I stopped worrying about who saw me. I was just in the presence of God. I have never felt anything like it. I don't even know how to describe the experience properly. It was like I was immersed in love and joy. I have heard many people tell me they love me. But now I felt like God was saying that to me. He said this even though he knew what I have done and what I still planned to do. I still cry about the moment when I think about it. I felt I was truly alive. God woke me up to the immense beauty of my life. It has forever changed me.

At that retreat, this young woman experienced the unsurpassable love of God. She welcomed the "vertical factor." Like the Samaritan woman in her meeting with Jesus at the well, she was touched by the love and understanding of God, and her heart opened as never before. She went home and at once threw away the razors with which she had contemplated taking her life. She experienced a dramatic interior reconfiguration, the gift of New Life in Christ. She has been able to put the self-consciousness and shame of her old life behind her, knowing that her present joy is of a greater order than her past pain. She attends Mass on Sundays and weekdays, along with weekly eucharistic adoration. She shares her joy with others, "going" enthusiastically to her family and friends as the Samaritan woman raced around her village filled with excitement. Several members of her family have joined the Alpha evangelization course because of her testimony of transformation. She serves the homeless. And, as she tells us, she looks ahead to the future not with dread but in expectancy that God will continue to care for her and lead her along.

Jesus beckons us to "come," and then he tells us to "go." The first keyword of the Great Commission contains this spiritual truth: before being apostles, we must become disciples. Only once we experience the transforming power of Jesus can we then become sharers of that life. For all of us, our apostolic zeal is inextricably tied to our experience of New Life, the authenticating core of our work of evangelization!

Make Disciples, Baptize, and Teach

Less of Jesus?

When stuck in a restless, unproductive sort of mood, we may be tempted to think: "I wish I was like one of the disciples who lived during the time of Jesus. If only I could have been next to the Sea of Galilee as Jesus passed through, close to the Master walking and speaking." We might be tempted to pity ourselves as having been born out of season—to consider the people of Galilee at the dawn of the first millennium as the truly fortunate souls of human history: they had Jesus himself, while we have to settle for the wisps of memory that have been passed down to us.

Our mood at such a time, however, is only that: a mood. We do not have less of Jesus. True, we cannot perceive him directly with our senses as the men and women who lived at the time of Jesus did. But they are not his sole contemporaries: he is also contemporary to us.

How so, exactly? One of the core paradoxes of Christianity is the interaction of particularity and universality. The incarnation is the primordial example of particularity. During his public life, Jesus proclaimed, taught, healed, and delivered. His action was limited to a specific time and place. There is no getting around the physical and temporal limitations of Jesus's earthly ministry; during the three years of his active ministry, Jesus reached only a particular group of people set in a particular time.

But the Father did not wish for the work of his Son to be limited to a specific time and place. What Jesus did once was meant to reach all. Jesus's mission was universal—possible and necessary to pinpoint historically—but nevertheless transcendent of the circumstances of the historical moment. A system of continuity, of handing on, of granting life and kinship with Jesus was a part of the plan from the outset. As Jesus proclaimed, taught, healed, and delivered people, he also gathered a group of disciples. He formed a group tasked with continuing his saving action throughout history. The historical events in which the first witnesses participated were meant to reach all people. Through the work Jesus's disciples initiated, the teachings, the healings, and the life of Jesus are made to be perpetually present with the same intensity and relevance.

The first community of disciples are those historically closest to the "wellspring," the resurrected body of Jesus. They draw the connection between the historical life of Jesus and subsequent generations. They are the Church as it springs forth, which we may define as the visible community of disciples that transmits the invisible life of God to all generations throughout history. Jesus is the wellspring, but out of him proceeds the Holy Spirit, which carries the life of Jesus across time and space. Dynamized by the Spirit, the Church brings the teaching and life of Jesus to us today. We partake of the same water "welling up unto eternal life" (John 4:14). In short, the Church makes Jesus's person contemporary to us. Accordingly, all of the actions of the Church are meant to put us into contact with the living Christ. Thomas Keating comments on the connection between the Christian tradition and the spiritual journey that each person undergoes:

> Christian tradition is not merely a handing on of various doctrines and rituals. It is the handing on of the "experience of the living Christ," revealed in the scripture, preserved in the sacraments, and received in every act of prayer, and present in a special way in the major events of our lives. Open and available to this presence, our lives will be transformed. The spiritual journey is a struggle to be ever more available to God and to let go of the obstacles to that transforming process. The gospel is not merely an invitation to be a better person. It is an invitation to become divine. It invites us to share the entire life of the Trinity.[3]

He is present to us in the proclamation of the word of God; he is present to us through fellow members of the body of Christ; he is present to us in the person of the priest in the sacrament of penance; and above all he is present to us through the Eucharist—Jesus's *real presence*, as we affirm. We do not have less of him, and we are not in an inferior position compared to those men and women who sat down next to him beside the Sea of Galilee: "Jesus Christ is the same, yesterday, today, and forever" (Heb 13:8). He is present to us *now*! And as we will see, to evangelize means to invite people to dive into this stream of water that transforms us.

Making Disciples

Disciples perpetuate the presence of Christ on earth. In this understanding of the Church, the work of the disciples is essential—not just for the fulfillment of their own conversion but in the very work of making Christ present. At the Mount of Olives, Jesus tells his disciples to carry out three essential actions, each of which follows upon their "going." He instructs them to make disciples, to baptize, and to teach. For the Church today

---

3. Keating, *Daily Reader*, 41.

(as then), these three actions converge upon one central goal: to make Jesus contemporary to us, to bring him alive within us. A crucial term to describe this goal spiritually is *incorporation into Christ*. All the things we do as a Church should engraft us more and more to Jesus, who is the vine to our branches (John 15:1–15).

The first action is to "make disciples." If in seeking to apply Jesus's words, we isolate this objective, we may feel daunted, like the responsibility is too big and too indefinite for us: What exactly does the task of "making disciples" amount to? Are we like personal trainers who are supposed to transform a sedentary desk worker into a marathon runner? Are we to be compared to the artisans who work tirelessly to make something beautiful from scratch—busily tinkering behind the scenes and then, all of a sudden, presenting the finished item for show in its immaculateness? "There you have it, complete and entire: a disciple!" Be assured: it is not a secret science or an incommunicable art form. To make disciples begins with a clear mandate: to proclaim the good news. The evangelization process starts with a bold proclamation of who Jesus is and what he has done for us. In Mark 16:15, another version of the Great Commission, Jesus says: "Go into the whole world *and proclaim the gospel* to every creature" (emphasis added). Go and proclaim! This is the first action necessary to carry out Jesus's instructions to make disciples.

When the proclamation is received with faith, it has the power to lead a person to become a disciple. Faith, biblically understood, means placing one's trust in Jesus. In the Gospels, those who demonstrate faith are those people who depend upon Jesus, who recognize his power, and who seek to give themselves over to him. Faith is a personal relationship with Jesus, a relationship that increasingly presses on to greater intimacy, trust, and self-surrender. To "make disciples" means then—through the proclamation of the gospel—to usher others into this rich, living relationship. The disciple-maker strives to teach people to grow in personal experience of Christ rather than to depend passively on the experience of others, to stand on their own two feet as disciples.

Baptizing

After the instruction to make disciples, Jesus tells his disciples to baptize in the name of the Father, Son, and Holy Spirit. The proclamation of the gospel aims towards the reception of baptism: we could say that in the heart of the addressed person, the proclamation stirs up potential energy that becomes kinetic in baptism. The faith aroused is "sealed" by the reception of the sacrament of baptism. In the case of someone who is already baptized but not practicing, the act of faith still has the effect of incorporation into Christ by unleashing the dormant grace of baptism. This "baptism in the Holy Spirit," often colored with all the drama and intensity of adult baptism in the early Church, awakens the person to spiritual reality, sometimes *as if*, sometimes *in fact*, for the first time.

Baptism, as the gate to the spiritual life, opens the way to reception of the other sacraments. Our faith grows and matures through fruitful reception of the sacraments of baptism, confirmation, and penance. In this respect, the second action of the Great Commission—*baptize*—implies the presence of what we call the sacramental system. To baptize is to initiate a person into the life of the Church and the current of grace that flows through it.

Teaching

The third imperative Jesus shares is to "teach them to observe all that I have commanded you." Especially given his use of the word "all," the responsibility implied here is immense. We get a sense of the scope of the disciples' mission: in their teachings, there is to be no subtraction from the teachings of Jesus. They are to be his representatives, completely so. They are the sheep sent among wolves: the plan of salvation for the world hinges essentially upon the fulfillment of their mission.

The Church, "built upon the foundation of the apostles" (Eph 2:20), continues this mission. The commandment to teach conveys the Church's understanding of the gravity of her role in the world. She is called to be the living voice of Christ in all times and places. She is called to proclaim a heavenly lifestyle to those wrapped up in the concerns of the world—and to form in her members a mindset grounded in the invisible world. She is called to be the bearer of the Christian worldview, which touches every dimension of human existence. The teaching of the Church reflects the fullness of the Christian life to which we are each directed. Through the initial proclamation of the gospel, we come to faith, but initial faith is not enough: it is but a raft on the seas. We require catechesis (*didache*). Through catechesis—catechesis intended to contact and transform our mentality—we build a ship suited for the waves.

Incorporation into Christ

Together, these three actions—to make disciples, to baptize, and to teach—point to a unified spiritual reality, an intrinsic dynamism, a meta-process of evangelization. This meta-process, directing each phase, is incorporation into Christ or, in short, life in Christ. Life in Christ is initially sown through the act of faith that follows upon hearing the good news. It is activated in an extraordinary manner through baptism. But then it continues to grow towards realization through a life of prayer, participation in the sacraments, and assimilation of the teachings of Jesus.

The parable of the vine and the branches of John 15 summarizes the spiritual phenomenon of incorporation. We are like branches that are only vital in connection to the vine. Jesus is the resurrected vine, and from his resurrected heart his life flows into us. Our growth from the vine begins through the act of faith and the sacrament of baptism, through which we are engrafted onto the vine. The sacraments and the teachings of the Church reflect the very aliveness and growth of the branches: through these means, divine life flows from the vine to the branches.

Incorporation into Christ can also be expressed as *growth in holiness*. We are not only called to become engrafted onto the vine but to draw more and more life from the source so as to bear more fruit. The Greek verb *meno* expresses the heart of this dynamic. It means "to remain," or "to abide." The verb appears repeatedly in John 15, nine times within seven verses. "Abide in me, as I abide in you," (John 15:4), Jesus says. "Abide in my love" (John 15:9), he adds, intensifying the meaning. This verb appears as well in Jesus's famous eucharistic speech in John's Gospel: "He who eats my flesh and drinks my blood *remains* in me and I in him" (John 6:57; emphasis added). We also see it in John's parting counsel to the disciples whom he calls his children: "And now, children, *remain* in him, so that when he appears we may have confidence and not be put to shame by his coming" (1 John 2:28; emphasis added). Moreover, *meno* sums up the inner sense of Paul's repeated characterization of his life *"en Christo."* "To live in Christ" is to remain in connection with Jesus, to draw one's direction and strength alike from him. To remain—to remain preaching and to remain praising the Lord—as Paul does, in the teeth of ridicule, injury, imprisonment, and the threat of martyrdom—is an indication of the depth of incorporation in Christ.

To remain, to abide, to live in Christ is the spiritual movement proper to our growth in holiness. We say "movement" because this is a form of remaining *with a motor*, a ceaselessly renewed positive striving towards union with Christ. It is made possible by Christ's indwelling—our abiding in him made possible only by his prior abiding in us. This communion, the human and divine participating in a unique union without either collapsing into the other, is the amazing glory of the Christian spiritual life. From this interior union and this union alone we "bear fruit that will remain" (John 15:16).

Saint Paul describes steadiness in bearing fruit as attaining "maturity in Christ" (Col 1:28). With maturity, we operate as not only disciples but also disciple-makers. Thus, we have traveled along the path opened up by the key actions of the Great Commission. From one angle, the visible elements and actions of the Church are ordered towards this end of "disciple-making"; baptism and teaching alike contribute to the formation of disciples. But from another point of view, no less valid, the disciple-making yields incorporation into Christ: the communication of the inner life of Christ so he can live in us and we in him, and so that through us he may be in the world. And on the last analysis, the view is all one: where disciple-making and incorporation into Christ merge into one another, we encounter the gaze of the missionary.

Evangelization Defined: Broad and Narrow

With the Great Commission as a backdrop, we can begin to define evangelization. The process of evangelization contains several stages, turning points, and nuances, and the action of evangelization cannot be described exclusively in terms of divine or human action but must account for the delicate synergy between the two. Nevertheless, following the biblical example of offering bold syntheses of complex teachings, we offer this starting point: *Evangelization is all that the Church does to incorporate people into the life of Christ.*

Pope Paul VI's *Evangelii Nuntiandi*, to which we have already referred, builds on this first leap. As the essential charter of the New Evangelization, *Evangelii Nuntiandi* takes up the task of defining evangelization. Paul VI provides a broad definition, focusing on the central mission and action of the Church:

> We wish to confirm once more that the task of evangelizing all people constitutes the essential mission of the Church. . . . Evangelizing is in fact the grace and vocation proper to the Church, her deepest identity. She exists in order to evangelize, that is to

say, in order to preach and teach, to be the channel of the gift of grace, to reconcile sinners with God, and to perpetuate Christ's sacrifice in the Mass, which is the memorial of His death and glorious resurrection.[4]

Note the elements of the Great Commission present: going out, making disciples, reaching all nations. Notice also how the notion of evangelization very quickly opens up to incorporate the whole life of the Church: preaching, teaching, the sacraments, and the Mass! We may usefully translate Paul VI's statement on evangelization to the realm of experience of Christ, circling back to John's vine and branches and the pivotal Greek verb *meno*. All the means of the Church are intended to draw us towards abiding in Christ at an ever-deeper level. As we are necessarily speaking of the "deepest identity" of the Church, to speak of evangelization is not only to encourage, persuade, or point towards participation within the Church. Evangelization *is* this participation itself—not merely an arrow pointing to Christ but the very life of Christ, shared through the instruments of the Church.

Returning to our guiding metaphor, we can think of evangelization as "inviting people to dive into the river of life that flows from the Risen Jesus and reaches us today through the Church." To evangelize means to invite people to plunge into the waters of New Life that heal, renew, strengthen, and transform us.

Incorporation into Christ describes broadly the entire process of evangelization that takes place in the individual soul through the Church. We may also speak of this process, however, in terms of its origin, casting back to the headwaters. We may define evangelization, thus, according to the first link in the chain: *To evangelize is to share the good news, or to proclaim the kerygma.* The kerygma, which we will continue to explore, is the term for the proclamation of the saving message of the gospel. This condensed definition of evangelization focuses on the heart of the message. In *Evangelii Nuntiandi*, Paul VI also validates this manner of thinking, when he writes: "There is no true evangelization if the name, the teaching, the life, the promises, the kingdom and the mystery of Jesus of Nazareth, the Son of God are not proclaimed."[5]

The etymology of evangelization supports this second approach to the concept. The word *evangelization* comes from the Greek noun *euangelion*, translated as "gospel" across the New Testament. It appears seventy-seven

4. EN, para. 14.
5. EN, para. 22.

times in the New Testament. At the outset of Mark's Gospel, we hear from Jesus the original usage that stands at the foundation of the notion of evangelization: "This is the time of fulfillment. The kingdom of God is at hand. Repent, and believe in the *gospel*" (Mark 1:15; emphasis added). *Euangelion* is what Jesus proclaims and what we are to believe in. The full sense of the word emerges from the role of the *euangelos*, or "good messenger." The good news brought by the *euangelos*, or the reward the *euangelos* received for bringing the good news would be the *euangelion*. From here it just came to mean "good news." To evangelize is to share good news. To be an evangelizer is to be a messenger of good news.

Considering the historical context, *euangelion* is a most emphatic, layered—and even provocative—word to use for the proclamation of Jesus Christ. In the Old Testament, the word (in verb form) refers to the good news of God's reign in the midst of Babylonian exile (cf. Isa 40:9, 52:7). The good news here is that the glorious God comes to deliver his people from Babylon and lead them back to Jerusalem. The good news of Jesus Christ builds upon, expands, and fulfills this notion from the Old Testament. The announcement of salvation through Christ is in direct conversation with the book of Isaiah: it is the realization of the long-awaited hope of Israel, the climax of the progressive revelation of God's reign, the ultimate manifestation of the character of the God who saves. But it is also unique—news in its very *newness*—surprising and transcending Israel's concrete expectations through salvation that comes from the crucified God-become-man.

The usage of the term in the Roman imperium gives us its provocative side. In the time of Jesus, *euangelion* indicated important news from the Roman Empire. The message a herald carried of a military victory in a distant land would have been announced as "good news." The birth of an heir to the emperor or the accession of a new emperor was also *euangelion*. This significance would not have been lost on the people hearing the gospel of Jesus Christ, living as they were under subjection in the Roman Empire. The good news of the gospel directly challenged the lordship of Caesar: the message of the evangelists is that this Jesus Christ—not Caesar—is their lord and king, and true lord and king of all in the Roman lands as well.

We are inheritors of both the Old Testament and the Roman streams. We stand in the tradition of the saving action of the God of Israel, and we also stand boldly behind the declaration that "Jesus is Lord," whatever opposition this declaration may arouse from conflicting powers. As evangelizers, we share the good news with the goal of leading people to faith:

we do this best with awareness of the nature of our inheritance. When we come and go forth, when we make disciples, when we baptize, and when we teach, we are enacting the Great Commission. We are doing nothing less than carrying out the instructions of Jesus Christ, our contemporary. We join the communion of saints at the headwaters.

CHAPTER TWO

The Kerygma: The First Link in the Chain

Introduction: "Good News for Me"

INFORMATION ASSAILS US. WE see too much and hear too much, too much we cannot make much of. We are like snorkelers in a frenetic, color-streaked sea; we hardly have the chance to follow a fish flashing by before another darting species makes a call upon our attention. We deal with input from beyond our control, and we also invite the assault. Information assails by way of the ubiquitous systems and social worlds in which we can't help but find ourselves—as well as through our own willed, privatized consumption. We are always grappling with our information intake, playing around with the valve, and, in truth, always ill at ease with the balance we have struck. We are forever wringing our hands about our management of the inflow, seeking a fresh approach in one way or another—whether readjusting our exposure to oversaturated spaces, vowing to limit our personal habit of purposeless scrolling, or changing our media loyalties to correspond with a shift in perspective. We are always asking ourselves: What should I let in? What should I pay attention to? The answer varies from day to day; admirable are those for whom the answer does not only vary but moreover *evolves* into configuration with a fuller grasp of truth and a deeper commitment to goodness. We monitor, we fret, we reassess, we wonder, and for all that we are never certain—nor should we be, given the difficulty—that we have gotten on top of this question.

When we are confronted directly with information that impacts *us* or, even more powerfully, with information that is *about us*, we turn insatiable. Say we hear one of the following statements: "Your exam results are back . . . We were talking about you the other day, and we all agreed that you . . . Your personality assessment revealed something interesting . . ." In each case, we want to hear the next word, with a sort of "want" different in kind and different in intensity from our desire (good-willed and broad-minded though we may be) to know, for instance, the present status of the endangered Galapagos tortoises. There is information that affects you, and then there is everything else. There is the easily tuned out din of interminable announcements at the airport, and then there is the one announcement, delivered in the same monotonous tone as the rest, that sends your heart racing: the final call for boarding on your flight, and one particular passenger, *you*, are being called to Gate C12. Our response to information can be understood as a function of the degree to which that information affects us personally. The information that really makes a mark is, invariably, *self-implicating information*. There is no exception to the rule: not only infatuated romantic partners but also sun-shy lab scientists respond as they do to their chosen interest inasmuch as they have become personally invested and implicated in what they process.

We now return to our encapsulated definition of evangelization as "sharing the good news," the good news Jesus called his disciples to carry out to all nations. Implicit in this charter is the conviction that the good news is good news for all. The evangelist is as sound as this conviction is strong in them, for the evangelist must believe in their heart, seek to convey by their speech, and transmit through their very person the universal significance of their message. By reaching the limit of the universal, it also penetrates to the level of the absolutely personal: if the gospel is for all, then the gospel is for each. The evangelist speaks a message for you, a message addressed to you: it is always your flight that is boarding.

Accordingly, each person who hears the proclamation in faith may affirm, "This is good news *for me*." The particularity of the gospel returns us now to the contemporaneity of Jesus. Jesus lived as a human being among human beings in his earthly life. Now glorified and resurrected, the Son of God lives among us without limitation of time and place, drawing us into communion with him *today*. Christ's presence empowers the gospel as an active and effective reality directed towards each person as a means of encounter. In his book *The Holy Spirit in the Life of Jesus*, Cardinal Raniero Cantalamessa writes of this feature of the kerygma, which as you recall from chapter 1, means the proclamation of the gospel:

> In the kerygma, "Jesus is Lord!," a mysterious transition takes place from history to "today" and to "for me." For it proclaims that the events narrated are not facts in the past, shut up in

themselves, but reality is still active in the present: Jesus crucified and risen, his Lord here and now; He lives by the Spirit and rules over all! Coming to the faith is the sudden, astonished opening of one's eyes to this light.[1]

If we define preaching the kerygma or evangelizing as sharing the good news, then we have to hasten to add that it is to share the good news *personally*, that is, in its personal significance, for the good of each individual recipient. When we share the gospel, we unfold the historical and eternal consequences of the coming of Jesus. We establish that this Jesus of Nazareth is alive today, that his love radiates out to meet us and uplift us today. But we present the message not in the form of a treatise—not as a kind of public lecture of interest for those who would like to acquire knowledge—but as an announcement. An announcement may be of objective interest, but it is also immediately and specifically relevant. The kerygma is an announcement or, to translate directly from the Greek, a *proclamation*. It calls for a response.

The Personal Dimension as Related by Jesus, Peter, and Paul

The Gospels, the Acts of the Apostles, and the Letters of Paul each help us understand the personal aspect of the kerygma more precisely. Jesus proclaims throughout the four Gospels, "The kingdom of God is at hand. Repent and believe in the gospel" (Mark 1:15). Jesus even says that his "purpose" is to preach this message (Mark 1:37). His purpose leads him to travel across villages with his disciples so as to encounter crowds in the open air, observant Jews in synagogues, and people of various backgrounds in family homes. He constantly pushes on to reach ever more listeners. What exactly does he tell them? How does he preach the coming of the kingdom? He communicates that, with his arrival, something new is happening. Sins are being forgiven (Luke 5:20; 7:48), and grace is made available (John 1:17). Evil is being conquered (Matt 12:29), and the kingdom is beginning to penetrate the hearts of many who will carry on his mission (Matt 13:33).

This is the character of the proclamation writ large, but individual stories illustrate best the personal effect of the proclamation of the kingdom. Matthew abandons his possessions to follow Jesus; the Samaritan woman,

---

1. Cantalamessa, *Holy Spirit*, 44.

we might say, abandons her resignation to the waywardness of her own heart. Both are forgiven, experience the wellsprings of New Life, and become instruments of Jesus's kingdom. So too, we can add Zacchaeus, who climbs up a tree to see Jesus above the crowds—and climbs down excitedly as Jesus calls him by name and invites himself to his house to dine. Zacchaeus repents, believes in Jesus, receives Jesus's announcement of salvation, and changes his conduct to accord with the change in his heart, offering to give half his possessions to the poor and to repay what he has extorted (Luke 19:1–10). Bartimaeus, the man born blind, is healed by Jesus, makes an act of faith in him, and then follows him along his way (Mark 5:46–52).

In each of these cases, Cantalamessa's description of the kerygma captures the thrill and depth of the exchange, the dramatic experience of becoming open to Jesus and the flow of the divine life through him. In each scriptural case, we observe through direct encounters with Jesus what Cantalamessa attests to as the power of the kerygma today, that is, "the sudden, astonished opening of one's eyes" to the light of Jesus. The encounters feature a common sequence. Jesus announces his divinity, either by innuendo or explicitly, and people believe in him. Jesus forgives their sins and offers New Life, which transforms those who assent to his influence. They then begin to follow Jesus, setting off with enthusiasm. The pattern unfolds repeatedly, leading as well to dramatic changes in the lives of relations of those Jesus touches directly, but it all starts with Jesus's catalyzing proclamation, that in him, the kingdom of God is at hand. Everything begins with the announcement that God is close.

→ A primира grande mistica !

∾ ∾ ∾

In the Acts of the Apostles, we observe this same pattern, yet with one key distinction: in Acts, the proclamation has been taken up in the power of the resurrection. The disciples hear Jesus's initial proclamation just as Zacchaeus and Bartimaeus do. They believe in him. They follow him. They experience forgiveness and sanctification. But then they go through the experience of the death and resurrection of Jesus, and the coming of the Holy Spirit. They are sent forth! Through their closeness to these events of salvation, they are privileged to understand what the Father has accomplished through Jesus. They pore back over the Scriptures, now grasping the interpretations Jesus gave of them; they reread salvation history through the lens of the paschal mystery. They are, in a sense, the supremely educated ones, but educated by experience as well as by the oral and written word. They are the great bearers of the wisdom of Christ, proclaiming that their experience of transformation can be shared by the people in their midst. In the Holy Spirit, they announce the essential message of Christianity: Jesus died for our sins, and he was raised for our sanctification (Rom 4:25).

We can hear in them the cry of "He has done it for me, and he has done it for you. He came to forgive you and heal you, as he has done for me. He wants to give you New Life, as he has given me New Life." During his earthly ministry, Jesus's kerygma was that the kingdom of God is at hand. In the Acts of the Apostles, we pass from Jesus's kerygma into the Church's kerygma, the proclamation in the Spirit of what Jesus has done for us and what we are called to do to receive him. The finest example comes in Peter's first discourse at Pentecost in Acts 2. The Acts account rapidly traces the following series of events: The disciples receive the Holy Spirit. Inspired by the Spirit, Peter courageously proclaims the kerygma to the crowd gathered in Jerusalem. Peter explains to them: "God delivered Jesus up according to his plan, and he was crucified at your behest [2:23]. Yet God raised Jesus from the dead [2:24], and we are witnesses to this resurrection [2:32]. God has made Jesus Lord and Messiah [2:36]." Peter then offers up the New Life that he has received to the crowd in front of him, promising the forgiveness of sins and the gift of the Holy Spirit through repentance and baptism (2:38). The gift, he explains, is not limited to them but also extended "to those far off" (2:39). About three thousand heed Peter's call and receive baptism (2:41).

Peter's proclamation stands as a definitive example of the kerygma because he lays out the two essential kerygmatic elements: the summary of the pivotal moments in the life of Jesus and the consequences for the lives of those addressed. In every age, to preach the kerygma is to preach the lordship of Jesus. In every age, the kerygma imparts the message that we are faced with a life-determining choice to either accept Jesus and travel along the way, or to let the opportunity escape us and return to our previous mode of existence. The kerygma communicates that Jesus died for each one of us—that he wants to give to each of us personally. As is evident from Peter's speech, the kerygma leads towards one goal: conversion. Faith in Jesus is its sole aim! The kerygma is sharp, pointed, purposeful, penetrating on the level of the human spirit like the beak of a woodpecker driving through the trunk of a tree. By the strength of the Holy Spirit, it is endowed with the power and vigor required to penetrate the toughest of initial resistances.

It is the opening move, the first link in the chain of the life of discipleship: nothing happens until the kerygma is preached.

∽ ∽ ∽

Saint Paul also represents a striking model of bold, succinct, and purposeful proclamation. He was a great evangelizer, a kind of force of nature as he traveled tirelessly; faced imprisonment; was whipped, beaten, and stoned; and still stood up to preach the kerygma before ever-changing, unpredictable audiences. Up until his death, Paul's momentous conversion experience on the road to Damascus remained at the root of his passion to share the gospel. At Damascus, Paul experienced that Jesus is real, that he is alive, that he forgave him, and that he called him to be his instrument. His experience and energy were singular, but Paul is also remarkable in the manner of his presentation, in his dedication to the core message. *He was able to get out of the way of the proclamation.* As he preaches Christ, he keeps the essential story of Jesus in the frame. He emphasizes that he does not stand before the crowds as a rhetorician or as a philosopher but rather as a messenger drawing upon demonstrations of the spirit and power (1 Cor 2:4). He recognizes that the difference—the distinctiveness—of the kerygma lies beyond the realm of human ingenuity or mere performativity.

When he does make use of his significant gifts of scriptural interpretation, he emphasizes the personal consequences of the passion, death, and resurrection of Jesus. He does not use his vast knowledge of the Torah to overmaster his listeners, but rather he returns to the two pillars of proclamation: the relationship to the life, death, and resurrection of Jesus; and the consequences for his listeners. For instance, in the Letter to the Romans, he connects the righteous faith of Abraham with the call laid upon his audience to believe in Jesus: "But it was not for him alone that it was written that 'it [his faith] was credited to him [as righteousness]'; it was also for us, to whom it will be credited, who believe in the one who raised Jesus our Lord from the dead, who was handed over for our transgressions and was raised for our justification" (Rom 4:23–25).

As quoted earlier, Cantalamessa summarizes the twofold action of the kerygma evident from the apostolic age—again, "the proclamation about Jesus" and "for our sake"—as he reflects upon the kerygma as the indispensable point of origin of the Church's various teachings:

What exactly is the content of this good news? . . . It is God's work in Jesus of Nazareth. But this definition is not enough; there is something more restricted, the germinative nucleus of all, which, compared with everything else, is as the plowshare to the plow: the sword of sorts that cleaves the clod, to let the plow trace the furrow and turn the tilth. . . . It is the instrument the Spirit uses to work the miracle of someone's conversion to the faith, to make someone be "born from above" (cf. John 3:3). I do not want to be the one to say this word; I leave it for Paul to say: "The word is near you, in your mouth and in your heart, that is, the word of faith that we preach [the kerygma], for, if you confess with your mouth that Jesus is Lord and believe in your heart that God raised him from the dead, you will be saved" (Rom 10:8–9). That word is therefore the exclamation, "Jesus is Lord," uttered and accepted in the wonder of a faith in its nascent state. The mystery of this word is such that it cannot be said "except in the Holy Spirit" (1 Cor 12:3). "As the wake of a fine vessel," as Charles Peguy would say, "becomes wider and wider until it vanishes and is lost, but starts at the point of the vessel herself," so the Church's preaching becomes wider and wider until an immense doctrinal edifice has been built, but begins at one point, and this point is the kerygma: "Jesus is Lord!" What the exclamation, "The Kingdom of God has come!" was in Jesus' preaching, is now the exclamation, "Jesus is Lord!" in the preaching of the apostles.[2]

Following the scriptural narrative from Jesus to Peter and Paul, we see the establishment of the main task of the Church: to proclaim the essential message that Jesus is Lord! With the Church, we proclaim that he reigns over sin and death, and he wants to reign over my life. When the Church declares this message in the Spirit, people come to faith and begin to participate in the Church's life; the whole Christian edifice is built upon the solid foundation of the act of faith that follows upon the preaching of the kerygma. Jesus is Lord! God raised him from the dead! He died for our transgressions, but he was raised to sanctify us. Do you believe this?

The Centrality of Discipleship

When we looked at the Great Commission, we reflected upon the correspondence between its core imperatives and the full trajectory of evangelization. We may view the principal action verbs of the Great Commission

2. Cantalamessa, *Holy Spirit*, 43.

(go, make [disciples], baptize, and teach) as representing the four central actions of the Church, arranged in a chronological sequence. "Go" signals the Church's movement out to all peoples; "make disciples," the sustained effort to evangelize, beginning with the kerygma; "baptize," the sacramental initiation into the Church as well as its full sacramental system; and "teach," the Church's ongoing catechesis and intellectual formation. This arrangement illuminates the priorities of the Church, the unfolding of its ministries. Still, we must make an important clarification: these four sequential actions are not equal. We can point to a hierarchy among the four actions, with one action in the leading position; or, better put, with one action as the orchestrating action, the action upon which the other three depend. In his book *Divine Renovation*, James Mallon identifies this central action:

> Jesus gave his nascent Church four tasks: go, make, baptize, and teach. Of these four imperatives, we find in the original Greek that one of them is a finite verb and three are participles. A finite verb is always the grammatical hinge of a sentence, and participles are verbal nouns that, although they qualify a sentence, ultimately make sense only in reference to the finite verb. So it is with the Great Commission. One of these verbs is the grammatical center of the sentence and thus, also, the theological center. . . . Which do you choose: to go, to make, to baptize, or to teach? Here's the answer: The finite verb is "make"—literally, "make disciples" (matheteusate). This task is the very heart of the Great Commission, and it is around the making of disciples that all the other missionary aspects of the Church revolve: the going, the baptizing, and the teaching. . . . We surely know how to baptize and celebrate all the other sacraments, but our one pastoral weakness, the task we struggle with the most, is that which lies at the very heart of Christ's commission to the Church: to make disciples.[3]

Mallon argues here that the hinge or foundation of the Great Commission is the task of leading people to become disciples. As we explored in the last chapter, discipleship requires faith, and faith flows from a personal relationship with Jesus. The first priority in the making of disciples is always relationship with Jesus Christ. Once people become solidified in their relationship, then their "going forth" constitutes the natural expression of their enthusiasm; baptism and the sacraments become live wires of faith—recognized and sought after in their power to transmit the divine life; and the teaching of the Church comes to occupy the center of the intellectual quest.

3. Mallon, *Divine Renovation*, 19–20.

Disciples bear fruit through mission and the works of mercy. Disciples are effective because they have received lesson 1: they have come to faith. They are able, willing, and eager to receive lessons 2, 3, and 4.

We cannot underestimate the significance of the personal assent of faith in bringing to realization all that the Church teaches and does. Even for longtime Catholics, the personal assent that comes from the heart—*real* assent rather than notional assent, according to John Henry Newman's parsing—cannot be taken to be a given. Yet this step is crucial. To participate in the life of the Church without making this assent of faith, to go through the motions without personal conviction, is to miss out on what the Church in fact provides. Many Catholics have grown accustomed to approaching the sacraments without having heard or digested the kerygma—no wonder that they receive the sacraments mechanically. The experience of sacramentality without the predisposition of faith is as fruitless as fixing one's eyes on a book while turning the pages in a pitch-black room: no one would argue that they had actually read the book once they had turned the last page. The lights must come on! The Church suffers a terrible deprivation when, in the words of theologian Peter Kreeft, her members are "sacramentalized without being evangelized," when lessons 2 and 3 (sacraments and teaching) are emphasized without making recourse to the principal lesson of faithful relationship with Christ.[4] As author Sherry Weddell remarks, the Church has too often accepted this state of affairs:

> We learned that there is a chasm the size of the Grand Canyon between the Church's sophisticated theology of the lay apostolate and the lived spiritual experience of the majority of our people. And this chasm has a name: discipleship. We learned that the majority of even active American Catholics are still at an early, essentially passive stage of spiritual development. . . . Rather, our fundamental problem is that most of our people are not yet disciples. . . . We learned that at the parochial level, we have accepted this chasm between the Church's teaching and Catholics' lived relationship with God as normative, and this has shaped our community culture, our pastoral assumptions, and our pastoral practices with devastating results.[5]

We must address this issue of spiritual development at its foundation. Later-stage action is useless without the initiating spark. Metaphors

---

4. See Kreeft, "Greatest Confession of Failure in Church History," 32–35.

5. Weddell, *Forming Intentional Disciples*, 11.

abound: we cannot flick at light switches while the circuit generator is off, nor drive a car without fuel. The predicament brings to mind a joke about an older person, gifted with a new computer by his children. He calls tech support and begins to complain, "I cannot get my computer to work, I am just staring at a blank screen. I told the kids that these fancy machines are more trouble than they're worth." The experienced tech specialist has an intuition of the source of the problem. She does not page through a troubleshooting manual, does not bother to dig into advanced techniques, but simply asks, "Sir, have you tried pressing the 'on' button?"

The Church needs to help people turn the power on, which begins with preaching the kerygma with the aim of making disciples. When the power comes on, when a person receives the kerygma with faith and starts to become an intentional disciple, both the person and his or her community experience a radical and welcome shift. Christianity becomes motivating rather than cumbersome, as the interior life receives a new imprint. Heidi, who received the kerygmatic proclamation through the Alpha evangelization program, is one such case. She was a self-identified "regular Catholic," but came to develop genuine spiritual ardor after receiving the kerygma. She described her renewed outlook:

> I had no idea that my life would change when I encountered the Holy Spirit. The Holy Spirit has penetrated my life to the extent that I now wake up in the middle of the night in prayer or song. Every day, I look forward to reading the Bible and praying. My conversion has also had an impact on my family, friends, and even strangers. I overheard one of my sons saying to a friend, "Yeah, my mom has this thing with the Holy Spirit now." Most surprising of all to me has been the powerful desire to be with Christ. At last Sunday's Mass, when the priest opened the tabernacle to return the unused consecrated hosts after communion, I was able to see directly inside the tabernacle, and I wanted to rush out of my pew and climb inside the tabernacle to be with Him. The Lord's presence has become an irresistible force in my life.

This kind of transformative individual action, when multiplied, engenders the shared joy and beauty of community life. When many people experience New Life, the kingdom becomes more than palpable; in fact, the work of the Spirit becomes obvious. The community grows to be full of people who believe in Jesus and grow in his likeness: new disciples look more like a continuation of the twelve and of the first community of apostles. The growth of a community through the proclamation of the kerygma is like the budding of a tree at springtime, with each fresh leaf representing the greening of the faith of someone who has received Christ in faith. In a community made up of many people configured to Christ, outsiders can breathe the presence of God among and through disciples, either drawing strength from the vitality of one particular member or taking in the assembly in its wholeness. Conversion begets conversion, and the community flourishes all the more. As Sherry Weddell writes in *Forming Intentional Disciples*:

> The presence of a significant number of disciples changes every-thing: a parish's spiritual tone, energy level, attendance, bottom line, and what parishioners ask of their leaders. Disciples pray with passion. Disciples worship. Disciples love the Church and serve her with energy and joy. Disciples give lavishly. Disciples manifest charisms and discern vocations. Disciples evangelize because they have really good news to share. Disciples take risks for the kingdom of God.[6]

The vision of Jesus is enacted through these very communities: to gather in, to reach out to all, and lead people out from their small selves into a culture of shared concern and mission! This is the aim of the New Evangelization: to form many communities of the kingdom. When we observe these communities coalescing, when we notice the previously-scattered unite—witnessing the formerly ideologically, politically, and economically divided group worship as one body—we recognize that the Great Commission bears fruit!

The Rediscovery of the Kerygma in the Church Today

The Sacramental Crisis

Now, this flourishing of Christian communities is no work of the imagina-tion, no unrealized dream; we write from the vantage point of being situ-ated in these vibrant communities. But we recognize that this is not the norm: on the whole, the Church has suffered a decline in membership in the West, which has led to anxious speculation. Even an exhaustive analy-sis of the reasons for decline in the Church in Western nations is unable to finally plumb the *spiritual* reasons for the exodus. Whether we speak of the rise of the technocratic paradigm in developed countries and the

6. Weddell, *Forming Intentional Disciples*, 81.

"this-worldly" mentality that often accompanies it, whether we speak of the Church's own failures to live out her mission and the scandals she has fallen into, or to the social displacement and psychological alienation that too often characterize our increasingly rootless lives, we only scratch the surface of the issue. We must speak in spiritual terms, and even here we are limited by our fragmentary perceptions, by our lack, as it were, of the ultimate knowledge of hearts, which belongs only to God.

One claim, however, can be established on solid ground, tautology that it is: when the Church fails to make disciples, the Church shrinks, and lately we have not been making disciples well. As the Church's strategy has focused on the administration of the sacraments, reception of the sacraments has fallen precipitously. Infant baptisms in the United States have dropped from roughly 1.089 million in 1970 to 411,000 in 2021; baptism of adults from 85,000 to 25,000; and Catholic marriages from 426,000 to 97,000.[7] Young people are also staying away from Mass: among young adult Catholics ages twenty-one to twenty-nine surveyed from 2014 to 2017, only 25 percent reported attending a religious service over the previous week.[8]

These statistics bring us back to awareness of the need for the New Evangelization. The Church must now be more intentional to evangelize those who are showing up and to reach those who are not. As the numbers indicate, in the present period we have no easy assurance that people will receive baptism, grow up in a Catholic context, and nurture the seed of faith. People must make a personal decision to follow Christ. Now more than ever, the proverbial phrase rings true, "God has no grandchildren, only children." Now more than ever, we must not merely rely on the generational passage of the faith but seize the opportunity to show others the way to become sons and daughters of the Father.

The Kerygmatic Response

How do we meet this situation appropriately, avoiding the extremes of apathetic resignation on one side and indiscriminate activity on the other? How do we relearn or reprioritize the need to make disciples? We have

---

7. CARA, "Frequently Requested Church Statistics." Though these low numbers are likely impacted in part by the pandemic that broke out in 2020, the numbers have been steadily dropping for decades. In 2015, infant baptisms registered at 693,000; Catholic marriages at 148,000; and adult baptism at 43,000.

8. Saad, "Catholics' Church Attendance."

already indicated the beginnings of an answer. We must start centered on Christ. We must treat sharing the good news as our priority. As we wrote in chapter 1, evangelization means proclaiming the gospel with the goal of leading people to faith, conversion, and life in the body of Christ, the Church. This definition leads to a more precise formulation of the term *kerygmatic proclamation*, which we have been circling. The word *kerygma* comes from the Greek *keryssein*, to proclaim. As the first link in the chain, the kerygma refers specifically to the initial and essential proclamation of the gospel message. As Saint John Paul II writes: "Kerygma is the initial ardent proclamation by which a person is one day overwhelmed and brought to the decision to entrust himself to Jesus Christ by faith."[9]

From John Paul II's definition, we can formulate the ideas we have been building thus far. *The kerygma is the initial ardent proclamation that leads to conversion.*

As the *initial proclamation*, the kerygma is not course number 201 but 101. It is not Omega (or even Beta) but Alpha. The kerygma presents what Jesus has done for us, clearly stated. Typically, catechists summarize the kerygma according to four parts:

1. Creation out of love

2. Brokenness by sin

3. Redemption by Jesus

4. Response by faith

The first three parts are the presentation of the narrative of Christianity. The movement from the third to the fourth part is especially important: the fourth (response by faith) calls for personal action from the hearer. We will explore these stages of salvation in greater detail, but for now we offer their recapitulation by Pope John Paul II:

> The subject of proclamation is Christ who was crucified, died, and is risen: through him is accomplished our full and authentic liberation from evil, sin, and death; through him God bestows "New Life" that is divine and eternal. This is the "Good News" which changes man and his history, and which all peoples have a right to hear.[10]

9. CT, 25.
10. RM, §44.

As an *ardent proclamation*, the kerygma must be carried out with faith, conviction, and the anointing of the Holy Spirit. Through ardor, the significance of what we communicate is effectively transmitted. The ardor may be our own but always as a borrowed good of sorts, as the outworking of the Spirit. In Cantalamessa's words:

> We cannot say "Jesus is Lord!" unless "under the action of the Holy Spirit," that is, unless we ourselves truly acknowledge this. If we say it, not "under the action of the Holy Spirit" but in sin, or disbelief, or out of habit, it remains a human saying which will not infect anyone: infection comes from contact with someone who has the illness, not with someone who talks about it.[11]

The final element of the proclamation is that the person is *brought to the decision to entrust himself to Jesus Christ by faith* or, stated succinctly, the person is *led to conversion*. Here we meet the goal of the kerygma as conversion, the great turnaround towards faith. In *Redemptoris Missio*, John Paul II makes this point:

> Initial proclamation has a central and irreplaceable role, since it introduces man "into the mystery of the love of God, who invites him to enter into a personal relationship with himself in Christ" and opens the way to conversion. Faith is born of preaching, and every ecclesial community draws its origin and life from the personal response of each believer to that preaching.[12]

Going back to the personal dimension, the completion of the directed address is the personal action for which it calls. The announcement that the plane is boarding may echo around the airport, but it is no more than background noise unless it causes someone to walk towards their gate.

The Kerygma and the Teaching of the Church

Because it is the initial ardent proclamation intended to lead to faith, the kerygma does not constitute its own resolution. The kerygma derives its value from the fact that it takes us somewhere. First, the kerygma orients towards baptism, link number 2. The next link, link 3, is the teaching of the Church, catechesis, or *didache*, which stands in complementary relationship to the kerygma:

11. Cantalamessa, *Holy Spirit*, 49.
12. RM, §44.

Through catechesis, the Gospel kerygma is gradually deepened, developed in its implicit consequences, explained in language that includes an appeal to reason, and channeled towards Christian practice in the Church and the world.[13]

Catechesis depends on the kerygma in order to have an impact, filling in the space in the mind and heart that is opened up by the proclamation. Stated in reverse, the kerygma is the precondition of catechesis. This is not only a theoretical assertion: we experience this phenomenon when we encounter the thirst to learn in those who have received the good news with faith.

Not only does the kerygma carry us up to the truth of the gospel, but it also remains with us: it is not a ladder that we kick away. This is because the kerygma permeates all that the Church teaches, for we are always being called to conversion of heart and to renewal of faith. As Pope Francis says:

We have rediscovered the fundamental role of the first announcement or kerygma, which needs to be the center of all evangelizing activity and all efforts at Church renewal. . . . This first proclamation is called "first" not because it exists at the beginning and can then be forgotten or replaced by other more important things. It is first in a qualitative sense because it is the principal proclamation, the one which we must hear again and again in different ways, the one which we must announce one way or another throughout the process of catechesis, at every level and moment.[14]

How to Share the Kerygma: The Importance of Entrance Doors

The mark of a special contribution in the sciences and humanities does not lie in the reaffirmation of what the community has already been saying; rather, breakthrough is characterized by fresh insight that opens the way to integration of what was not assimilable within the previous paradigm, the explanation of the fact for which previous models could not account. The fruit of the breakthrough is the development of a theory that permits for the expansion of the horizons of knowledge. Analogously, in evangelization, the great work to be done is achieved through an expansion of reach—in this instance, through connection to people who previously did not find a place within the Church. As evangelizers, attentiveness to the

13. CT, 25.
14. EG, 164.

largely unseen group outside of the present communion is central to our vocation. To meet this group, we can first embark upon the work of reimagination of our church communion from the outside. Are we inviting to the outsider? Do we offer formal programs, also with less demanding events that help people feel welcome to explore faith?

An evangelizing community must not only preach the kerygma well but must also provide entrance doors that bring people in to hear it. The Church's mission is to provide catechesis, to distribute the sacraments, *and* to provide instances wherein people may hear the kerygma. To offset the pattern of kerygmatic neglect we described earlier, churches must be intentional in this domain; they must have a bureau, so to speak, dedicated to evangelization. We must prioritize evangelization. Crucial to this initiative is the sustained awareness that Christ does not just live in the midst of the present assembly for its own good, but rather lives in the midst of the assembly in order to go beyond it. As Pope Francis has shared, Jesus stands at the door and knocks, but we have to imagine him not only as knocking on the door of our hearts but also as knocking from the inside of the front door of the church, asking to be let out and move onto the streets and to the margins. Whether knocking from inside or outside the church, Jesus asks us to open our doors.

As a Church, we need to facilitate access to Christ through doors of entrance. What are some viable entrance doors or pathways to hearing the kerygma? One is the personal presence of people who have been evangelized. This door is opened through the personal invitation that a committed Christian makes to someone in their life who is not committed to the same degree. We believe that, above all else, friends inviting friends is the most effective mode of evangelization. Sharing faith with friends is an organic process that can nonetheless be cultivated. Saint John Henry Newman refers to the power of personal influence, which we will discuss in greater detail in chapter 7.

To encourage and develop brave faith sharing, we can instill a culture of sharing *on the inside* first. People become more comfortable going out with their story once they have shared with others who can identify with and validate their experience. From this starting point, we can encourage people to write down and deliver their conversion story. This is not to say that sharing faith is a technical art form like public oratory or debate; as we pointed out, Saint Paul took great pains to make clear that testimony of faith is most decidedly *not* this kind of transmission. However, we should

acknowledge the positive role of preparation, training, and habit formation even when counting upon the inspirations of the Holy Spirit. Once
people are confident in their ability to share, then they are often more
willing to follow the Spirit where it leads them in spontaneous encounters.
Sharing personal testimonies within the community has the secondary
effect of bringing people of faith into closer relationship with one another,
helping all parties to recognize common sufferings and consolations in
people whose backgrounds might otherwise remain more obscure than
illumined in each other's eyes.

A community of faith also does well to develop organized forms of
entrance doors. We can seek to multiply occasions wherein the kerygma
is preached, including conversion retreats and evangelization courses.
These events resemble the preaching of Peter and Paul in front of crowds.
If one-on-one faith sharing is analogous to fishing using a pole, then there
is also a place for fishing with a net. In the Saint John Society ministries in
Oregon, for instance, we offer eight initiation retreats for men and women
of the Spanish-speaking San Juan Diego community. The renewal that takes
place through these retreats is invariably a fortifying experience, for priests
and laity both: we witness not only dramatic spiritual healings but also a
contagious, uplifting spirit of gratitude that instills loyalty to Christ and to
community. Evangelization courses are likewise entrance doors that gather
groups prepared to hear the kerygma. At each of our Oregon parishes, we
host two Alpha courses each year—one course for college students and one
for adults of all ages. These courses provide a step-by-step process of evangelization; the kerygma unfolds through focus on particular "kerygmatic
questions" such as "Why did Jesus die?" and "What is the Church?" The
courses also feature a retreat in which we call for the coming of the Holy
Spirit upon the participants; in this way, the kerygma becomes profoundly
experiential, its power unleashed.

Entrance doors are the first essential opening to the kerygma, but we also
must reiterate the proclamation once inside. When Pope Francis calls the
kerygma "qualitatively" first, he points to its double character as both first
link in the chain and the constant spur to deepening life of the Spirit; it
stands at both the beginning of the chain and the beginning of the next
movement forward, whatever that movement may be. A thriving faith

community is accordingly imbued with an evangelistic spirit in all its activities: in sacramental preparation, in the Sunday homily, in faith formation courses, and in catechesis, the kerygma should always be surfacing. The kerygma must be everywhere present in our veritable house of faith—not just the subject of the striking painting near the front door but a motif in each room of the home. Wherever we operate in the Church—addressing bishops or catechizing children—we cannot simply assume that our audience knows Jesus; we must always be returning to the announcement of the glory of his lordship.

The kerygma gains in wealth when it is preached and coordinated with other elements of faith. It stands alone at the beginning—like a sudden trumpet blast—but then it later becomes coordinated with the whole variety of instruments that belong to the Catholic orchestra. The specific definition of evangelization (the sharing of the good news) and the broad definition of evangelization (all that the Church does to incorporate people into Christ) are helpfully distinguished—but only to be brought together on the final analysis. The only way to start is through the kerygma, and the only way to continue is to integrate the kerygma within the full life of the Church.

— CHAPTER THREE —

Conversion: The Entrance
of the Vertical Factor

EVANGELII NUNTIANDI CONTAINS UNEXPECTED insights into the nature
of evangelization, but in chapter 7, Paul VI states the obvious and irre-
futable: "Jesus Himself, the Good News of God, was the very first and
the greatest evangelizer."[1] He was the greatest evangelizer in terms of the
depth of his sacrifice, as he gave all for the sake of his mission. Whereas
we invariably struggle to bridge the distance between persona and person, to unite inner desire and outer task, for Jesus there was no gap, no
distance, between self and mission. He was, in a way that fallen human
beings cannot replicate, *entirely whole and unreserved* in his evangelization. He was the greatest evangelizer because he was what he preached,
the kingdom of God in person.

So, there exists this spiritual distinction to his ministry, but humor us
for a moment as we speak in more material terms. He was a great evangelizer based on results; he was a great evangelizer because he led thousands of
people to conversion. We have already enumerated the stories of converted
souls in the Gospels: there are the first disciples, among whom we have the
account of the dramatic calls of John, Andrew, Peter, Philip, and Nathanael.
There is the hesitant Nicodemus, who drew closer to Jesus as the Gospel of
John unfolded. Also recall the Samaritan woman at the well, the adulterous
woman who received Jesus's mercy, and the man born blind whom Jesus
gifted with sight, all of whom came to faith through Jesus. Lazarus, Mary,
and Martha received his friendship and gave their loyalty; Mary Magdalene
developed a love strong enough to remain through the crucifixion. Behind
each of these people, unique in their call and path to discipleship, we can

1. EN, para. 7.

fairly presume a collection of others who encountered Jesus in various circumstances and were transformed by him.

As we have seen in the Great Commission, Jesus does not only spread the gospel. He also initiates others into his mission. Jesus sends the members of the Church to lead others into an experience of New Life. In reading the Acts of the Apostles, the sheer number of people who experience conversion stands out amidst the narrative of the establishment of churches. We hear: "The word of God continued to spread, and the number of the disciples in Jerusalem increased greatly" (Acts 6:7); and "Yet more than ever, believers in the Lord, great numbers of men and women, were added to [the apostles]" (Acts 5:14). Acts portrays a community grounded upon New Life that adds strength to strength, drawing in untold numbers of people to experience New Life in Christ directly.

The same action present through the ministry of Jesus and the apostles rings true for the growth of the Church beyond the apostolic age. On many occasions, God bursts into action; he *irrupts* into history and unleashes his Spirit. Unforeseeably, God acts through a charismatic figure and/or movement to trigger the flow of new groups and new peoples into the Church. In the first three centuries after Christ's earthly life, the wave into the Church came through the efforts of the first missionaries, who spurred the conversion of erstwhile pagans. In the Middle Ages, the mendicant orders (led by Saint Dominic and Saint Francis) renewed the Church as they traveled across Europe in imitation of Christ's peripatetic lifestyle. In 1520, the apparition of Our Lady of Guadalupe stood as the fountainhead of the surge of the millions who came to faith in Mexico.

When we notice the increasing secularism of the present age, and especially if we take up an implicit mental model of history as a patterned, programmatic, and regular unfolding, we may be tempted to think that these movements represent the rise of a great curve that is now rounding downwards: the curve of the rise and fall of Christian faith. We are tempted to think that the momentum of Christian fervor is now in irretrievable decline. It may very well be that the age of Christendom (wherein general society adopts the Christian narrative vision as its own guiding worldview) is over, but Christendom is not synonymous with Christianity, and we cannot mistake this transition for a necessary diminishment in the work of the Holy Spirit in and through the Church. Adherence to this negative thesis would constitute the failure to see and trust the novelty and unpredictability of the action of the Holy Spirit.

Considering its transcendence, the Spirit's action does not translate into direct earthly-historical patterns: the exact workings of the Spirit remain a mystery hidden in eternity, a mystery governed by divine freedom. We can testify to the Holy Spirit, but our knowledge is partial; we are only ever chasing the Holy Ghost, which blows where it will. One thing we can say for certain is that the fertility of the Holy Spirit defies expectation. Think of the unpremeditated and sudden power that characterized each of the aforementioned historical turns. As stated in *From Christendom to Apostolic Mission* by Monsignor James Shea:

> What sociological survey could have predicted the conversion of an ancient and sophisticated civilization at the hands of a small group of uneducated laborers? What numerical analysis could have surmised the explosion of the monastic movement? Or the conversion of all the pagan peoples of Europe? Or the appearance of a Saint Francis and his thousands of followers in a few short years? Or the apparition of Our Lady of Guadalupe and the conversion of Mexico?[2]

What is to prevent one of these sorts of movements from happening again today? Why couldn't we expect the same outpouring of the Spirit in our present context? As we see people leaving the Church in droves, we can feel ourselves pushed towards discouragement. A spirit of defeat can sneak in and gradually conquer the hearts of the members of the Church. Even missionaries and ministers in the Church become vulnerable to losing confidence. But we cannot let go of our trust in the action of the Holy Spirit. God is not bound by any natural principle of growth and decline; the supernatural is not susceptible to our earthly logic. The Holy Spirit can transform individual lives—and the whole course of history—at any time. We must remain open to the possibility of great numbers coming back to faith through conversion, even as we do not depend on this development. We must preach from a spirit of victory, which is not reducible to head counts, nor even to the experience of successful missionary labor, but remains anchored in the already inaugurated victory of Christ.

2. Shea, *From Christendom*, 39.

The Waves of Evangelization:

In four remarkable Advent sermons, Cardinal Raniero Cantalamessa lays out the four waves of evangelization that have featured at different moments in Church history.[3] Each wave possesses a particular form, a group of protagonists, and an audience that came to be included within the world Church. The four waves are delineated as follows:

1) The spread of Christianity in the first three centuries, lasting up until the Edict of Constantine inaugurated a closer alliance between Church and empire. During this wave, Christianity gained a foothold thanks to the bold, enthusiastic missionary initiative of itinerant prophets, who first went out from Jerusalem into the Mediterranean world and unto the limits of the Roman empire. As Christian communities began to emerge, so too did more coordinated efforts of evangelization, with the community standing as the "evangelizing subject" and the local bishop directing.

2) The sixth to ninth centuries, the time of the reevangelization of Europe following the Barbarian invasions. Monks carried the Catholic faith to kingdoms that had previously given their assent to the Arian heresy in modern-day England, Holland, France, and Germany, as well as to territories never previously exposed to Christianity. This era culminates with the conversion of the Slavic peoples of Eastern Europe through the work of Saints Cyril and Methodius, who developed the Slavonic alphabet to teach the Scriptures to the peoples they encountered. The steady leadership of monks in these wild and unpredictable mission fields makes evident the centrality of contemplation in evangelization.

3) The sixteenth century, with the discovery of the New World and the subsequent conversion of the peoples of the Americas. The leaders of this wave were the friars: the Franciscans, Dominicans, Augustinians, and Jesuits. Considered today, the relationship between colonization and evangelization raises serious questions. Nevertheless, we can affirm the good of sharing Christ: Pope John Paul II, for one, recognizes that there were both lights and shadows in this period but expresses joy that today the people of the Americas make up a lively, dynamic, and numerous contingent within the Church.

4) The present age, in which the Church has committed to a reevangelization of the secularized West. For Cantalamessa, the laity stand as the protagonists of this period. The Second Vatican Council of 1962–65 proclaimed the universal vocation to holiness; the laity, who make up the vast majority of the Church, are called in the present situation to reach out and influence workplaces, families, and cultural institutions.

---

3. See the numbered listings of Cantalamessa's Advent sermons in the bibliography.

Why Study Conversion?

In this chapter, we examine the experience of conversion, seeking to understand how people come to faith. We start from the foundation of the missionary identity of the Church. Put pointedly, the underlying mission of the Church is to prolong the experience of New Life in Christ. The first priority must be to lead people to take on this New Life through discipleship. As missionaries, we must learn how this process unfolds. Much in the way that a psychologist comes to understand the stages of personality development through a mixture of empirical data and concrete self-reports from clients, we study and contemplate the phenomenology of conversion: we collect the data of the lives of the saints, and we pay close attention to the development of the spiritual life in those to whom we minister. By focusing on these realms of experience, not only do we grow in knowledge, but we also increase our wonder at the work of God. At some point, we must get beyond a merely theoretical theology to notice God working in the here and now.

Each conversion is a powerful manifestation of the action of God. As Saint Thomas Aquinas argues in the *Summa theologica*, if we consider goodness from the point of view of the end-product attained, the conversion of one person is even greater than the work of creation (!):

> A work may be called great in two ways: first, on the part of the mode of action, and thus the work of creation is the greatest work, wherein something is made from nothing; secondly, a work may be called great on account of what is made, and thus the justification of the ungodly, which terminates at the eternal good of a share in the Godhead, is greater than the creation of heaven and earth, which terminates at the good of mutable nature. Hence, Augustine, after saying that "for a just man to be made from a sinner is greater than to create heaven and earth," adds, "for heaven and earth shall pass away, but the justification of the ungodly shall endure."[4]

Witnessing to God's action is a great encouragement for evangelizers *and* a great tool to help bring about the conversion of the evangelized. Testimony is not superfluous; it serves the purposes of the kingdom. The book of Tobit reminds us of the need to testify to God's action: "Proclaim before all with due honor the deeds of God, and do not be slack in thanking him. A king's secret should be kept secret, but one must declare the works of God

---

4. Aquinas, *Summa theologica*, q. 113, a. 9.

and give thanks with due honor" (Tob 12:6–7). In the book of Revelation, we hear the perhaps startling impact of our thanks: Satan is conquered by the testimony of witnesses to Christ's salvation (Rev 12:11).

In our own faith experience, we notice how testimony of conversion brings New Life in Christ into the open. In the Saint John Society, at the end of our Holy Spirit retreats we provide an open mic opportunity among the retreatants. People have experienced the coming of the Holy Spirit— for many in amazing and profound ways—and we give them the chance to proclaim what has happened within them. We set up a large circle of chairs (normally we have between fifty and seventy people present), and we leave the microphone standing right in the center of the group. Perhaps you consider this to be cruel! To those who are naturally reserved, the microphone might seem like it is bobbing out in the middle of a cold and rough sea. Truly, it is an act of bravery for anyone to wade out into the center, remove the microphone from the stand, and share their experience. But invariably person after person makes their way to the microphone and shares a testimony. Many confess that they never could have anticipated that they would share candidly in front of a group of relative strangers but that, in the moment, they felt a prompting that they could not resist. People tend to tell us afterwards that they were "blown away" twice in the retreat: first by the Holy Spirit coming to touch and awaken their hearts; second, by the power of the Spirit expressed through the people who stood up to share. What appeared at first as a singular (and perhaps rare) phenomenon—the Holy Spirit moving *me* intimately, personally, supernaturally—comes to be seen as taking place in so many more men and women (without compromise of personal touch and uniqueness). This type of experience epitomizes the way we come to know God's glory in a communal context. Through the shared manifestation of New Life, we learn of the magnanimity of God, the depth and breadth of his action, and the very gratuity of his love.

Moreover, we see our own spiritual journeys reflected in other people—down to our struggles and our sins, down to, that is, specificities. If we hear that God has healed someone from depression even when they thought healing impossible, then we can find a source of hope in our own mental health struggles; if God can break through our neighbor's loneliness and nurture a new point of view, then, of course, so too can God work renewal in our personal circumstances. As people share their conversion stories, we find God mysteriously speaking to our own heart. We find strength for the journey, encouragement to remain steadfast even amidst our own backsliding and long-lasting battles. And as we discover ourselves to be more connected and more similar to one another than we had fathomed, we awaken as well to the reality that we make our way in the Church as brothers and sisters. We awaken to nothing less than our solidarity.

The Conversion of Saint Paul

The Church places great emphasis on stories of conversion. Many of the feast days of the Church take place on a conversion day: We have the feast of the conversion of Saint Paul on January 25, and John Henry Newman's feast day, selected for the day of his conversion to Catholicism from Anglicanism, is celebrated on October 9. In celebrating their conversions, we likewise celebrate the action of God—the irruption of God's power into a human life, the moment when God's grace brought about a new creation in Christ. We look also to the accounts of conversion to gain inspiration for ourselves: among Catholics, *The Story of a Soul*, by Saint Therese of Lisieux; *Confessions*, by Saint Augustine; and *Apologia Pro Vita Sua*, by John Henry Newman, among others, are especially prized.

Saint Paul's story, which is written into sacred Scripture, can be used as an illustration of the features of conversion as well as a mirror to understand our own personal conversion. This event was so important for Paul that he relates the story of his conversion and references it at many points in his writings. In the Acts of the Apostles (cf. 9:1–19; 22:3–21; 26:4–23), in Gal 1:10–17, and finally in 1 Cor 15, he speaks of Jesus's appearance to him that changed his life. We will draw on each of these accounts, but at this point, we recommend that you pick up your Bible and read through the narrative of Acts 9:1–19. From the text and the additional testimonies of Paul's conversion, we highlight eight major elements of conversion—in correspondence with the number the church fathers deemed the number of salvation (the seven days of creation and Sabbath plus the coming of Christ).

Prehistory of Conversion

By taking into view the prehistory of conversion, we indicate that faith necessarily emerges from a prior period of development, however hidden the work of this period may be. If Paul first encounters Jesus on the road to Damascus through an apparently out-of-the-blue visitation, still Jesus must have been preparing his heart before that moment. In the following chapter, we will study how the act of faith is typically preceded by several thresholds of conversion—graduated breakthroughs into deeper levels of readiness to accept the gospel. People usually start at the threshold of curiosity: they may research the faith, and then, as they grow in desire for more tangible engagement, seek to meet other Christians. For Saint Paul, we observe a great irony to his "curiosity," in that his initial interest in Christians and Christianity was impelled by harsh judgment, even hatred: before his conversion, what he learned about Christians and Christianity only contributed to his passion to persecute them! Did Paul's rage towards Christians perhaps include an aspect of misguided and destructive defense against God's grace-filled invitations, a kind of mysterious hardening against God's love? We can only speculate, but in any case, whether a person is moved to opposition or moved to openness, we can always find a story of gestation that precedes conversion; the period is no less a period replete with God's grace.

Through the term *prehistory of conversion*, we also gesture towards the development of all the abilities, talents, and characteristics that a person possesses prior to conversion. When God transforms a life, he does not write upon a tabula rasa. On the contrary, grace presupposes and assumes (takes in and takes up) the features already present: grace enters into the personal background of experiences, education, and unique gifts, the elements we might sum up as the "horizontal factor" to meet the vertical factor of the inbreaking of grace. Divine grace assumes the education of Paul—his training in the law in Jerusalem under the revered teacher Gamaliel, as well as his acquaintance with the Stoic philosophical ideas of his time. Grace assumes and transforms his passionate nature, the very nature that led him to persecute Christians prior to his conversion. God uses his universal character as an instrument, his status as a zealous Jew, a Roman citizen, and a speaker of Greek. It is the same story with all the saints: after reading the *Lives of the Saints* and committing himself ardently to Christ, Ignatius of Loyola does not cease to be related to the Ignatius wounded on the battlefield; his personality is still recognizable as his own. Rather, now his self-glorifying ways as a mercenary soldier have given way to zeal for the greater glory of God as a self-professed soldier of Christ. So too when Christ comes to you: he transforms the person he meets; there is nothing generic about his action.

Time and Place

Each conversion is a determinate event, a determinate event that takes place according to a spiritual *and* historical order. As with any historical event, it may be expressed according to the coordinates of space and time. With respect to space: Paul was moved to conversion on the outskirts of the city of Damascus (located in modern-day Syria), two hundred miles outside of Jerusalem. Imagine how meaningful that place must have become for him: he might have kissed the ground every time he returned there.

Taking Paul's experience on the road to Damascus as our index, we can imagine the "personal Damascus" of saints and historical and biblical figures. In the Old Testament, people would build an altar wherever God manifested himself. We have the classic example of Jacob's altar, which Jacob constructed in the place where God revealed himself to him as he was fleeing his brother Esau (Gen 35:7). Saint Augustine's Damascus would have been the garden at Ostia where, in tears, he surrendered his will entirely and experienced the ineffable light of God filling his soul. Nathanael had his fig tree, Zacchaeus a certain sycamore. We often find that, as we reflect on the site of our Damascus, we can summon a rich, detailed memory of the place where we first prayed in earnest or where we first felt the presence of God—and that all the details we recollect are infused with a certain poignancy.

We also tend to remember the month or season; where the sun hung in the sky if we were outside, or how dark the night if the sun had already fallen; if we were at home, whether before the house had awoken, after the lights had been turned off, or in the midst of the activities of the day. This is the second of our two coordinates: time. In the account of his conversion in Acts 22, Paul says that it was about noon when "a great light from the sky suddenly shone around me" (Acts 22:6). This hour is particularly significant symbolically, because it is near the peak of the sun's strength: the implication is that the light of the Risen Jesus is stronger than the light of the sun at its zenith. And as with our own stories, it is an indication of the precision of the memory of the event, its lasting significance, the trace it leaves in the heart. The apostle John, most excellent in love of Jesus, remembers the hour when he first saw Jesus in the flesh, "at four in the afternoon" as the Gospel reports.

God's Initiative

The great light shone "suddenly"; Paul was caught unawares. This history-shaping moment that led Paul to a radical personal reorientation came at the initiative of God. This is the nature of relationship with God: most fundamentally, we witness God's search for the person and the person's participation or collaboration within the leading action of God. Even as we recognize our volition in the spiritual journey, we must bear in mind the always antecedent action of God that directs the steps we take towards him. As Pope John Paul II writes in *Redemptoris Missio*, "Conversion is a gift of God, a work of the Blessed Trinity. It is the Spirit who opens people's hearts so that they can believe in Christ and 'confess him.'"[5] (cf. 1 Cor 12:3). All conversion implies this supernatural guidance and foundation.

We might absorb this idea according to the image of a father and his young daughter running and playing together in the park. The father runs ahead, calling out to his daughter. The child, spurred on by her father's energy and encouragement, follows along, laughing and clumsily making her way behind him. Keeping an eye on his daughter, the father slows down so that his daughter can catch up. Once she reaches him, he bends over, smiles at her, and picks her up, and the game starts all over again. God's first creative movement in relationship to us gives us the impetus to begin taking steps towards God—and it is only ever through God's infinite patience and love, as he stoops down to our level, that we continue ahead on the journey. We respond to God's love with a love that is borne of this same love. We are called before we come running. As Jesus says, "It is not you who chose me but I who chose you" (John 15:16).

Freedom (Vulnerability)

Paul is bowled over by the radiance of the light of Christ. He falls to the ground—the tireless religious leader suddenly now blinded, weak, and without defenses. Caravaggio's great painting *The Conversion of Saint Paul* captures the incapacitation of Paul, including even the detail of his helmet rolling on the ground next to him. In the painting, he opens his arms wide in a gesture of surrender, a fitting image for the great reversal of Paul's spiritual position. Even as Paul speaks of his zeal to follow the ancestral traditions of Judaism, we can detect the self-will that drove his life, as he "persecuted

---

5. RM, §46.

the church beyond measure and tried to destroy it" (Gal 1:13–14). As he was knocked over by the light of Christ, he was on his way to continue this persecution, set upon arresting Christians in Damascus. He may have seen himself as a servant of the law, and he may have been operating within the matrix of religious authority, but he doubtless took the law of God into his own hands. In this pre-Damascus life, he held the reins—and how tightly he gripped them! He was convicted of his judgments and took himself to be the director of significant action. Paul was in charge.

It is disputed whether Paul was riding a horse on the road to Damascus. The distance between Jerusalem and Damascus suggests that a horse would have been suitable for the journey, although the text makes no mention of Paul falling from a horse, just of his falling down. Regardless, we are not contradicting the inmost reality in saying that Jesus takes Paul down from his horse. From this moment forward, Paul has been unseated as the director of his own life. We see the same message related by the narrative detail that he was led away by the hand because he could not see (Acts 19:8). Paul does not resist; he allows himself to be led to where Jesus tells him to go. Paul chooses to serve God in freedom, but he is first shown the limits of his own strength.

God's entrance into our self-directed lives constitutes the painful upheaval of our former values and projects. We cannot have it another way. As our past approach disintegrates, we may be shaken, we may be thrown, but when we get up, we must make the free assent of our will. In so doing, we allow ourselves to be led, even against the urge to bolt in fear at what is asked of us or frustration over our vulnerability. God takes the initiative, yet we must open our hearts and allow God to change them; no matter the providence that lays our path, we still have to walk. As we set off, we discover joy and the renewal we may not have known we needed. Pope Benedict XVI captures the dual aspect of faith, its dependence upon God as well as the free assent of each person, when he says:

> Faith is a gift of God, but it is also a profoundly free and human act. The Catechism of the Catholic Church says so clearly: "Believing is possible only by grace and the interior help of the Holy Spirit. But it is no less true that believing is an authentically human act . . . contrary neither to human freedom nor to human reason" (n. 154). Indeed, it involves them and uplifts them in a gamble for life that is like an exodus, that is, a coming out of ourselves, from our own certainties, from our own mental framework, to entrust ourselves to the action of God who points out

to us his way to achieve true freedom, our human identity, true joy of the heart, peace with everyone. Believing means entrusting oneself in full freedom and joyfully to God's providential plan for history, as did the Patriarch Abraham, as did Mary of Nazareth. Faith, then, is an assent with which our mind and our heart say their "yes" to God, confessing that Jesus is Lord.[6]

Vision from Heaven (Heavens Are Opened)

The voice and light that come down from heaven break open the hard shell of Paul's former existence. Just as the heavens are opened above Jesus in his baptism, the heavens are opened over Paul on the road to Damascus. As we pointed out, the breakthrough is symbolic of God's initiative and free action: when the heavens are opened, God intervenes. This free action of God—this objective irruption of God—corresponds on the human-subjective pole to a breakthrough in human consciousness. As the heavens are opened, Paul's mind is opened. He perceives what he did not perceive before; he sees Jesus and Jesus sees him. The experience is intensified by the fact that Jesus speaks his name twice (calling him Saul, the Hebrew variant of the Roman name Paul). In being named and seeing Jesus as he is seen, Paul realizes that Jesus is alive and that Jesus knows him personally. We can look to Pope Benedict XVI again, who trains our focus on the encounter with Christ that constitutes the center of Paul's conversion event:

> The average reader may be tempted to linger too long on certain details, such as the light in the sky, falling to the ground, the voice that called him, his new condition of blindness, his healing like scales falling from his eyes and the fast that he made. But all these details refer to the heart of the event: the Risen Christ appears as a brilliant light and speaks to Saul, transforms his thinking and his entire life. The dazzling radiance of the Risen Christ blinds him; thus what was his inner reality is also outwardly apparent, his blindness to the truth, to the light that is Christ. And then his definitive "yes" to Christ in Baptism restores his sight and makes him really see. . . .
>
> St. Paul was not transformed by a thought but by an event, by the irresistible presence of the Risen One whom subsequently he would never be able to doubt, so powerful had been the evidence of the event, of this encounter. It radically changed Paul's

---

6. Benedict XVI, "General Audience" (Oct. 24, 2012).

life in a fundamental way; in this sense one can and must speak of a conversion.[7]

The marvels of any conversion event gather themselves around and reveal the essence of what God seeks to give us: an encounter with the living Jesus. It is an encounter in which we come to know that he knows us, and through which we learn to believe in him as the meaning and measure of our existence, for the dramatic opening of the heavens simultaneously constitutes the opening of our awareness to the presence of God in Christ.

Mercy

Jesus sharply confronts Paul in his sinfulness. The first thing he says to him is "Why are you persecuting me?" Jesus is direct, but this confrontation does not spell condemnation. It is a confrontation that emanates from his merciful heart, for Jesus seeks to forgive Paul, to lift him out of his ignorance and wrongdoing. Correction here is rightly perceived as just another side of the love of a God who seeks to see his creature restored and brought to holiness.

We cannot forget that Paul was previously convinced of his righteousness. Jesus introduces Paul to the depth of his guilt, identifying for him what he had been doing all along—not serving God as he supposed but persecuting the Son of God. This insight grants us a powerful reading of the shape of God's mercy. We fall short when we understand God's mercy as functioning to let us off the hook for the sins we had already more or less accepted, like the police officer letting us go without a speeding ticket when we demonstrate how sorry we are for having broken the law.

Rather, the very action of his mercy is to show us our sins as we had not seen them before (there is a kind of mercy also in being alerted to our unsafe habit of driving), while still giving us hope in this situation; the mercy of God changes our relationship to our sinfulness, both in leading us towards the honest recognition of our guilt and in supplying the strength to get beyond it through the forgiveness offered. By grace, we see sin not merely as an idea or notion we attempt to wrap our minds around but as a serious, urgent, and charged reality, an existentially destructive element that we must face. By grace, knowledge of sin reaches our heart, moving us with awareness of our many nos to God's will. But this bracing

7. Benedict XVI, "General Audience" (Sept. 3, 2008).

awareness does not leave us disconsolate: Jesus's promise of forgiveness prevents our self-consumption in sorrow; we are uplifted even amidst our self-knowledge by the gift of his love. In fact, Saint Paul testifies to Christ's generous treatment in his First Letter to Timothy, "I was once a blasphemer and a persecutor and an arrogant man, but I have been mercifully treated because I acted out of ignorance in my unbelief. Indeed, the grace of our Lord has been abundant, along with the faith and love that are in Christ Jesus" (1 Tim 1:13–14).

Paul writes to Timothy that Jesus exercised patience with Paul as an "example for those to come" (1 Tim 1:16). He wants Timothy to see through his case the essential form of God's merciful action on behalf of future disciples: the sharp and bracing encounter of the light of Christ with the darkness of the sinner—an encounter, that, despite its starkness, does not lead to the sinner's rejection but rather to an opportunity for change. Mary Magdalene faces her wayward past, Thomas his destabilizing doubt, Matthew his selfishness and greed. For the person who meets Christ, the experience is often accompanied by a sentiment of repentance—sorrow over the previous way of life and resolution not to return to the same path in the future. Jesus sees the sin, forgives the sin, and calls to a higher standard; we receive his word of reproof, repent, and seek to move forward in his love.

Mediation of a Person

Jesus works through others for the good of Paul: In concert with his appearance to Paul on the road, he appears to the disciple Ananias in a vision and instructs him to baptize Paul. Initially, Ananias resists, deterred by the reports he has heard about Paul's persecution of Christians in Jerusalem and his plans to make arrests in Damascus. Jesus reassures him that Paul is an instrument of his kingdom, and Ananias goes out to Paul. When Ananias lays his hands on him, Paul recovers his strength. Notice that Jesus reveals himself directly to Paul on the road to Damascus, yet he chooses to restore his sight and initiate him into discipleship through the means of one of his servants. Jesus brings Paul's faith to completion—endowing him with the gift of the Holy Spirit—through the mediation of another person.

Ananias stands as a reminder of our reliance upon other people in the process of conversion. In many conversion stories, we see people come to faith because of the witness or influence of another believer. To reflect back to two of our featured saints: as a young man, Saint Augustine was amazed by the substance of the preaching of Saint Ambrose, especially the conformity of his life to his preaching. Augustine first attended Ambrose's sermons to learn about the art of rhetoric, but he found himself most impressed by the rhetoric's grounding in a lived-out truth. Saint Francis Xavier was led to a fruitful life of mission through his relationship with Saint Ignatius as a student. Such is the humility inherent to life in Christ—the need for instruction by way of the example of others—that we can scarcely find a saint not guided into their vocation by an outstanding spiritual influence. It is important to remember that God brings us into configuration with him through human relationships! We can and should identify our Ananiases, the people who have helped us along the path to conversion.

But we also realize that God empowers these relationships behind the seemingly accidental means by which we come close to him. Through the relationship Ananias establishes with Paul, we look into the process of the construction of the household of God, a household built on the apostles and composed of fellow citizens (Eph 2:19–20). In his relationship with Paul, Ananias is a symbol of the Church. Jesus sends Ananias as a member of the Church, no less than as a representative of him. As Paul meets Ananias, he is meeting the Church. Ananias's presence signals that Paul embarks not just upon a personal but also a corporate experience. As he receives the Holy Spirit from Ananias, he receives too his membership in the Church—the Spirit-guided body directing the person who mediates the gospel to him. Paul's journey began when Jesus appeared to him and asked, "Why are you persecuting me?" By *me* Jesus refers explicitly to his Church, the body of Christ. Paul's journey reaches a resolution when he joins this very body he had once violently opposed—joining now, in the words of Ananias, as a "brother" to those he persecuted (Acts 9:17).

Sacraments: Heaven Lives in Me

The conversion experience is brought to fullness by baptism—not completed for good, for conversion is ever ongoing, but brought to its proximate goal by the spiritually objective gift of rebirth in Christ. In the Acts narrative, we read about a continuous stream of actions once Ananias meets Paul: Ananias lays his hands on Paul, and Paul receives the Holy Spirit; Paul then regains his sight, and immediately he is baptized; he eats and recovers his strength (Acts 9:17–19). It is through the gift of the Holy Spirit that Paul's eyes are opened. His illumination is a symbol of the gift of New Life tied to baptism. "Receiving baptism" and "joining the Church" are two ways of expressing the same reality. Paul journeys forth until he joins the body that he once persecuted; we could also say that he journeys until the life that he once sought to extinguish, the life he encountered on the road to Damascus, comes to reside within him. And now that the life of Jesus is within him, he will operate from a new way of thinking, of feeling, and of loving. This whole transformed self will be given over to the new mission with which Paul has been tasked. When Paul says, "I live, no longer I, but Christ lives in me" (Gal 2:20), he makes clear the real abiding presence of the indwelling Christ.

We observe in Paul the form of the Catholic experience of New Life, which is realized by the reception of the sacraments. As previously discussed in the analysis of the Great Commission, the first link of the kerygma connects to the second link of the sacraments and intentional discipleship. Through the sacraments, and in a special, initiating way through baptism, the indwelling of God becomes more firmly rooted in us. We read in Pope John Paul II's encyclical *Redemptoris Missio*:

> Conversion is also joined to Baptism because of the intrinsic need to receive the fullness of New Life in Christ. As Jesus says to Nicodemus: "Truly, truly, I say to you, unless one is born of water and the Spirit, he cannot enter the kingdom of God" (Jn 3:5). In Baptism, in fact, we are born anew to the life of God's children, united to Jesus Christ and anointed in the Holy Spirit. Baptism is not simply a seal of conversion, and a kind of external sign indicating conversion and attesting to it. Rather, it is the sacrament which signifies and effects rebirth from the Spirit, establishes real and unbreakable bonds with the Blessed Trinity, and makes us members of the Body of Christ, which is the Church.[8]

While in baptism we are born anew, in confirmation, the Eucharist, and reconciliation this life is ratified, developed, and renewed. The Catholic understanding of conversion is powerful precisely because it transcends the level of an emotional experience: our account of conversion remains grounded in the objective work of redemption enacted through the sacraments.

---

8. RM, §46.

Application: Writing and Sharing Your Story

Sharing your personal journey of faith can be a great means of evangelization. We are each responsible for telling the world what God has done in our own life. You may never know who will be impacted by your testimony or how God will use your witness in someone's life. It is helpful to write your conversion story down—and to keep your story fresh as your vision of God's work in your life evolves.

How to write it? For a general structure, you can answer these three questions successively:

1. What was I like before I encountered Jesus? What kind of a person was I socially, spiritually, and emotionally? You may want to introduce a unifying theme, either touching upon a relatable aspect of your experience or an accessible theological idea. (For example, you could talk about possessing a familiarity with Christ but no personal knowledge of him, your experience of loneliness, or your unsatisfied spiritual hunger.)

2. How did I encounter him? What happened? What events or people came into my life that led me to encounter Christ? Perhaps your conversion has been more gradual. Try to describe the process with attention to the details of the situation that led you to Christ.

3. How is my life different now? What are the fruits of New Life that Jesus has brought to my life? What changes have occurred in my life? How am I living out my relationship with Jesus?

Tips for Sharing Your Testimony

- Avoid using loaded words and phrases that could separate you from those who are not familiar with a specific religious vernacular. Try to hear yourself from the perspective of someone less familiar with Christianity.

- Avoid extremes. Try not to come across as a perfectly realized saint. At the same time, however, don't dwell on struggles and failures such that the darkness of your account overwhelms the light.

Be Specific but Respectful with the Details You Choose to Include.

- Specific details make your story memorable; to be specific does not take your story out of the realm of universal human experience but rather gives the authentic stamp of life that helps people connect.
- If you plan to use people's names, make sure to ask in advance to see that they are ok with you doing so.
- Understand your audience's maturity level and cultural sensitivities. As with delivering a talk, you are best off knowing where your audience is coming from.

Do Not Aim to Preach or Teach Explicitly.

Focus on your own life. Only use Bible verses that directly involve your story. Your job is not to teach others the catechism but to share your own first-person account.

—— CHAPTER FOUR ——

Prehistory of Conversion:
Thresholds of Faith

IN THE JEWISH PHILOSOPHER Martin Buber's great essay "Education," Buber stresses the pivotal responsibility of the educator to know his or her students. According to Buber, the educator must meet each student not from a vague idea of the student's starting point but rather from genuine awareness of the student's experience of the world. He writes, "The person whose calling it is to influence the being of persons . . . must experience their action ever anew from the other side. Without weakening the action of their own spirit, [the educator] must at the same time be over there, on the surface of that other spirit which is being acted upon. . . . Only when the educator catches himself "from over there," and feels how it affects [the student], how it affects this other human being, does he recognize the real limit of his teaching, baptize his self-will in reality, and make it true will."[1] Buber might as well be expressing a core facet of the task of evangelization: the charity-driven movement into the space of the other person, a humble movement undertaken in order to encounter and respond to another's unique outlook. This habit becomes a profoundly important discipline of evangelization, requiring both attentiveness and self-restraint. The missionary is like the owner of a dress shop who must bring out from a vast inventory the wedding dress suitable for the bride. The owner cannot simply pick the fancy, new dress just arrived from abroad, but must discriminate, matching the person to the available dresses—placing, if need be, the specificities of the person above any prior preferences and tastes. Likewise, the missionary must seek to bring out from their storehouse of knowledge and experience

---

1. Buber, *Between Man and Man*, 100.

the story, the self-disclosure, the word, the verse, or the event most appropriate for their interlocutor.

To help us land "on the surface of the other spirit," as Buber recommends, we can educate ourselves on the realms through which the spirit passes—what we call "the thresholds of faith." As we saw with Saint Paul, prehistory of conversion marks the path to the act of faith; before people make an explicit commitment to Christ, they have already undergone a process of initial seeking that leads them to the decision to drop their nets. Here, we aim to impart a fundamental grasp of these thresholds of conversion. We cannot neglect personal familiarity as the ultimate means of reaching another person, but each threshold points in a certain direction, indicating a tool or approach that will be most effective for sharing Christ. Knowledge of the thresholds ensures that we end up in the right neighborhood; it remains our specific mission to find the home, knock on the door, and enter. The thresholds, identified by Intervarsity Christian Fellowship, progress according to this sequence: Trust, Curiosity, Openness, Seeking, and Discipleship. We will look at each in turn, drawing on the work of Sherry Weddell of the Catherine of Siena Institute, who has developed the thresholds in her study of Catholic evangelization, *Forming Intentional Disciples*, which we recommend for deeper analysis of the topic.[2]

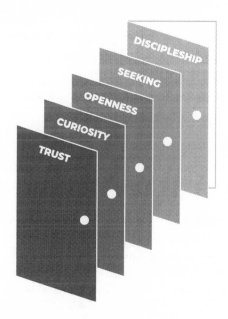

2. Weddell, *Forming Intentional Disciples*, 125–84.

Threshold 1: Initial Trust

At the first threshold, a person possesses a degree of trust in or has a positive association with Jesus Christ, the Church, a Christian believer, or something identifiably Christian. In many cases, trust resides in a relationship with one particular Christian friend or family member whose witness of faith exercises attraction.

For the evangelizer, the trust threshold, still far short of active personal faith, provides the opportunity to build a bridge. The tricky issue here can be the relative depth of trust; sometimes we find a very limited trust that still throws up partitions between Jesus and the Church, between a close friend and the body of believers, or between personal spirituality and institutionalized religion—maintaining confidence in one side of the dichotomy but not the other. However, we often discover great strength even in this limited region of trust: strength in enduring memories (say, of a Christian retreat), in sincere affections (relationship with beloved companions), or inspiring teachings (perhaps a pillar of Catholic social teaching). It is important to be attentive to personal disclosure to discern where the bridge across the river can be laid, upon which outcropping of land the person is comfortable stepping towards—whether to begin for instance with prayer, or the person of Christ, or the intellectual tradition of the Church.

Saint Justin Martyr's notion of seeds of the Word (*logos spermatikos*) connects with this threshold. Recollecting his own journey to faith through Greek philosophy, Justin recognized that when people come to faith, they build upon aspects of the truth they have already known. Justin proposed that Christ has sown seeds of truth far and wide and across time, such that even people alive before the coming of Christ could have rightly been called Christians.[3] Though these seeds may be partial and mixed with error, they are genuine starting points for dialogue and building blocks in the process of conversion. Seeds of the Word can be implicitly held in the form of practices or more consciously held in the form of ideals. Today, we could classify as evidence of seeds of the Word practices as various as sustainable use of goods, humanitarian aid to war-torn regions, service to the poor in urban centers, and humble neighborhood responsibility. The principle of the unity of God among Muslims, the family values lived out by Mormons, and the inherently moral-religious dimension of human psychology attested by the work of contemporary depth psychologists count as

---

3. Justin Martyr, *1 Apol.* 46.

well. In *Lumen Gentium,* the constitution about the Church in the Second Vatican Council, we have reference to the same concept through the term *praeparatio evangelica.* As the document states, "Whatever good or truth is found among [those who have not attained an explicit knowledge of God] is looked upon by the Church as a preparation for the Gospel."[4]

We nurture trust by making room for relationship. Avoiding defensiveness, judgment, and forcing the issue, we should validate the seeds of the Word we detect and continue to open doors to reach closer contact. People are not so much led forward by a ready supply of flawless answers to their questions as by uncomplicated compassion and acceptance. At the trust threshold, we are still in the stage of "pre-evangelization," wherein we are cultivating the predisposition to receive the gospel. Accordingly, patience and steadfastness are the watchwords of the trust stage.

Threshold 2: Curiosity

We can imagine the transition from trust to curiosity as a shift of the gaze: the eyes begin to lift and look up to the object of faith. At the threshold of curiosity, a person finds him or herself intrigued by Jesus Christ. At this stage, people want to know more about Jesus's life, his teachings, and the Christian faith that professes him. Curiosity varies in intensity: some people will ask a Christian friend a question, while others will empty bookstores of their works on apologetics. Curiosity often pertains chiefly to the intellect, but it can also be a sentimental curiosity (developed through finding a grandmother's rosary), an aesthetic curiosity (provoked by the beauty of a Catholic liturgy), or an interpersonal curiosity (stimulated by the peace of a Christian). Each of the transcendentals—including beauty and goodness as well as truth—has the power to stir curiosity. People are moved at the stage of curiosity—moved, in fact, by the pull of divine love in its various manifestations—but they are not yet open to personal change. They are looking, not yet acting. They want to know more about the one at whom they are looking, and they will often say so.

We can meet the direct interest in Jesus Christ with the direct proclamation of the good news about him. We must make it our concern to familiarize people with Jesus and expose them to the life of the Church, conveying our own attachment to Jesus and the inextricable connection between Jesus and the Church. We should do this passionately rather than

4. LG, 16.

disinterestedly! As Sherry Weddell puts it, "Whenever we treat Jesus as a 'topic' within the faith as opposed to the 'whole spiritual good of the Church' (CCC 1324), or as a 'belief' among other beliefs instead of as Lord, Head, Bridegroom, Savior, and Elder Brother, we profoundly distort the faith and communicate an impersonal or institutional understanding of what it means to be Catholic."[5]

The reality of Jesus alive among us is greater than any idea can convey. Jesus possesses the power to break through the veils of daily life, surpassing all prior conceptualizations. Beyond previous notions of the essence of our reality, he supplies the extraordinary penetration of his teachings. Out past the categories of worldly virtue, the holiness of his disciples shows forth a new standard of goodness. And beyond the various musical and visual forms that attract our admiration, the beauty of the liturgy directs our attention to the author and archetype of all that amazes us. The truth, goodness, and beauty of Jesus have the capacity to draw the attention of the soul out of boredom, routine, and resignation and towards something new.

Even as we point to Jesus as the ultimate horizon—creatively drawing the circumstances of daily life into relationship with Christian teachings—we should not cede our focus on the person in front of us. We should answer the questions they ask about Catholicism, but we should be asking questions even more than we are answering them—stimulating further curiosity rather than merely satisfying the curiosity already present. People are now beginning to construct the picture of life as a follower of Christ, turning their curious gaze not only towards Jesus but also towards a concrete community of faith. This can mean getting to know the community, not necessarily becoming a part of it. We are still not yet asking for action at the threshold of curiosity: both of the first two stages are essentially passive. A distance remains. Imagine the person watching a passing parade through their bedroom window; it has caught their eye, and even perhaps absorbed their attention, but they are not ready to leave the comfort of their home and join the stream.

Threshold 3: Openness to Change

Here at the third threshold, a person acknowledges openness to the possibility of personal and spiritual change. A mirror is picked up; the beholder turns to look at themselves, as they begin to contemplate their

5. Weddell, *Forming Intentional Disciples*, 143.

transformation into a new self in Christ. Openness is the stage where many people get stuck. It is an especially difficult transition because the next step implies the risk of leaving behind the familiar and embracing a new form of life. We often hear that people resist change—of all kinds; we are attached to our habits and to the lifestyle we know. This is a natural fact. As for the spiritual plane, Saint Ignatius teaches that the enemy seeks to cloud awareness of the good that will come from conversion; Satan hides from view the benefits and blessings that God will endow us with once we give up our present position, and he exaggerates the anticipation of pain at what we will be giving up. The truth is that it is painful to break a habit or let go of an attachment, but this process, like the refinement of metal by flame, constitutes a beneficial purification. We break out, and the life of God breaks through!

If we are more settled in our faith, we may struggle to empathize with the existential fright that a person faces at this threshold. We may have eyes only for the polished metal on the other side, while the person at this threshold may be focused upon the flame! As Weddell writes, "The one on the verge of openness can feel as if he or she is teetering on the edge of an abyss, while the lifelong Catholic wonders what all the fuss is about."[6] To leave home for an extended stint in a foreign country, to break off a long-lasting but counterproductive relationship, to contemplate a major career change, all of these experiences intimate something of this vertiginous position. Not only are these events analogous to the situation of this threshold, but they can also trigger the step from curiosity to openness: major life events—births, deaths, and upheavals of all sorts—often lead people to this threshold. An experience of the gravity and depth of existence can provide the courage to move out from comfort and custom and onto this exposed ground.

As missionaries meeting people at this stage, the mystery of human freedom confronts us. Why do some people resist change, even when they recognize that they are wedded to unhappiness? Why do some argue for Christianity with the rigor of a trained theologian and the passion of a preacher, only to inexplicably turn their backs on involvement within a faith community? Why, on the other hand, do certain people suddenly plunge in—after having given every indication of insurmountable resistance to the Church? At this threshold, we cannot give in to the temptation to try to force people along. Rather than pressing in anxiously, we can make clear our availability and willingness to accompany. We should be like the doctor

6. Weddell, *Forming Intentional Disciples*, 156–57.

of a woman who is nine months pregnant: we are on call and ready to support, perhaps checking in occasionally, but we are not frantically leaving messages every five minutes to see whether the time has come yet. If we are questioning why the "seemingly easy" step forward is not being taken, we can convert our restlessness into fruitfulness by offering intercessory prayer. And when we are called upon, we can help the person to interpret their journey, nudging towards awareness of the work of God bringing them ever closer to the heart of Christ.

Thresholds 4 and 5: Spiritual Seeking and Discipleship

The threshold of seeking marks the transition from the essentially spiritually passive stages of preparation to active pursuit of God. This is a threshold not just of progress but of *forcefully breaking through a threshold*—of breaking free from an exclusively receptive stance into action! Sherry Weddell aptly terms this stage "dating with a purpose." Seekers are forthrightly asking, "Are you the one to whom I will give myself?" As with consideration of marriage, implications for time, money, and relationships all come to the fore: the obligations and transformations attendant to following Christ become manifest. The seeker is engaged in an urgent spiritual quest, attempting to determine whether he or she can commit to Christ and his Church. At this stage, people tend to be asking more directed questions, reading and/or researching, and spending time within a Christian community. The seeker may start to make some behavioral changes but usually very much by way of anticipation: the final commitment to Jesus has not yet been enacted.

Our role at this juncture is to increase our availability, offer invitations to suitable events, and provide resources. We can help to instruct the seeker in methods of prayer and invite them to attend corporal and spiritual works of mercy. The whole dialectic of evangelization is a dialectic founded upon desire: we are at every stage meeting the desire that we recognize, and we are pointing towards the next forward movement beyond the consummation of the present desire. The key is to ask for the right motion at the right pace, like the trainer who establishes the proper course between extremes—not sapping the athlete's confidence by coaching too much nor enabling them to plateau by aiming for the same goal day after day. At this threshold, the next forward movement is the step into deeper union with the body of Christ. We seek to include people at this stage in the general life of the community—and once they appear ready for the leap, we should not hesitate to invite them to jump.

At the point at which they leap, they have entered the stage of discipleship. We follow Weddell's definition of discipleship as the free commitment to become a follower of Jesus Christ, with all the changes, sacrifices, renunciations, and commitments that this entails. This is a great arrival, and a great, liberating surrender of the self: the disciple confesses the lordship of Jesus and adores him as Savior. The disciple not only surrenders to Jesus as Lord but also becomes like Christ. As we read in the Gospel of Luke, "No disciple is superior to the teacher; but when fully trained, every disciple will be like his teacher" (Luke 6:40). Sometimes, there is a clear sacramental marker of the passage to discipleship, like baptism or confirmation. But this is not the only way to solidify discipleship, which is why as missionaries we must provide opportunities that facilitate the act of faith, including retreats, Alpha courses, and prayer nights.

Transformation continues after initial conversion; there is no flat ground in the spiritual life. When we follow Jesus with our whole hearts, we go from grace to grace, from glory to glory. As _Redemptoris Missio_ puts it, "Conversion gives rise to a dynamic and lifelong process which demands a continual turning away from 'life according to the flesh' to 'life according to the Spirit' (cf. Rom 8:3–13)."[7] Our spiritual growth comes to be expressed through two predominant, mutually reinforcing outlets: service and evangelization. Healthy Catholic communities find ways to make use of the gifts of new disciples—gifts plainly visible prior to conversion as well as latent gifts stirred up by the Holy Spirit. For service, we can encourage people to share their talents with members of the community—and then find creative ways to develop their talents within the community. For evangelization, we can help people to gain greater insight and clarity about their story of coming to Christ as a means of reaching out to others.

"Conversion gives rise to a dynamic, and lifelong process which demands a continual turning away from 'life according to the flesh' to 'life according to the Spirit'."

Redemptoris Missio

---

7. RM, §46.

Three Types of Conversion

In his book *Fulfillment of All Desire*, Dr. Ralph Martin speaks of three types of conversion.[8] This schema helps us to place the shape of our own spiritual journey as well as those on the road. See which type applies most closely to you.

Development: "Sometimes people who are baptized as infants simply grow up in an atmosphere of faith, gradually maturing into a life of deep holiness and mission. While healing and purification are often still needed for people in this situation to make progress (sometimes quite a bit), there is no marked experience of an awakening or conversion from life apart from God. Such was the case of Therese of Lisieux and Francis de Sales. . . . They were blessed with family environments of faith and solid instruction, and simply matured into the life of holiness and the special missions God gave them."

[?]This was my case.

Awakening: "On the other hand, there are others who, while they may be living some measure of Catholic life, often do so with lukewarmness or significant compromise. People in this situation seem to be stuck serving two masters or simply blind or unaware of what the call to holiness really involves, and don't make much progress on the spiritual journey. The Lord often gives grace to people in this situation to awaken them to a fervent Christian life. Teresa of Avila testifies that she was among the lukewarm whom the Lord needed to awaken in order for her to begin again to make significant progress on the spiritual journey."

Conversion: "There are others living further away from the Lord who need more than an awakening. . . . Some of these may be living in the depths of unbelief or in deep bondage to serious sin. Some may have practiced their faith at one time to some degree but for various reasons turned away. Some may have never heard the gospel or been baptized or embarked on the spiritual journey. For people in these situations, God in His mercy gives grace sufficient to bring about conversion or reconversion. Saint Augustine testifies that such was his situation."

As we accompany people through the thresholds, we should remind ourselves of just how much is going on within them; we should remember that the process of conversion is nothing less than the process of God working out the salvation of a soul. Let us meet this situation with reverence

8. Quotations under "Three Types of Conversion" are from Martin, *Fulfillment of All Desire*, 17–18.

and patience. Because the spiritual life entails purification and renewal, we must get used to time scales and processes of a different rhythm than suggested by our default notion of efficiency-driven activity.

To return to the life of Saint Paul: Paul realized that his experience of conversion meant the initiation of a New Life, and he acted accordingly. As he shares in Galatians, after his baptism he went to Arabia for three years—a kind of extended spiritual retreat—before traveling to Jerusalem to consult with Peter and begin ministry (Gal 1:15–18). We will see people go through periods of apparent inactivity, as well as periods of inspiring development: let us be prepared for both. The primary rule is attentiveness to the person journeying towards discipleship. As we follow along the stages, we see the kinds of actions indicated at different points. At the level of trust and curiosity, we are in a time of sowing prudently, not overfertilizing the soil but giving what the situation demands. Without the progression towards openness, there is very little we can do; we must respect the will of the person we encounter. At the stage of openness, we can come forward in readiness for fuller accompaniment. And at the seeking stage, it becomes appropriate to intensify the relationship, to push forward, so that the person can clearly recognize the demands of discipleship and reap the fruits of greater conformity to Christ.

—— CHAPTER FIVE ——

Persuasion: Evangelization as a Positive Reality

MOTIVATION IS SOMEWHAT LIKE health: we do not pay much attention to it when we have it, but when we don't, we struggle mightily—trying this and that to land on a solution. And like health, motivation is a precious component of our overall flourishing. When people are motivated, they move from one project to another: they may start a diet, study for a difficult exam, begin dating, or train for a competition. Their interior drive moves them towards a certain goal and provides them with the strength to overcome obstacles along the way. Endowed with this sense of forward movement, even day-to-day activities give off a freshness that eludes the person lacking willpower; we could say that for the motivated person, the ordinary is readily perceived as extraordinary, whereas for the unmotivated, even the extraordinary gets dragged down to the level of the mundane.

This principle is equally true for those on the road to faith. If someone lacks fire for the things of God, we cannot marvelously implant a desire within them: some people are so closed that even the saints would preach to them in vain. In the classic parable of the sower, Jesus makes the analogy between various kinds of soil and the preparedness of a person's heart to receive the gospel. The seeds sown along the path, along rocky ground, and amidst soil choked with thorns do not bear fruit; lacking interior readiness and availability, the heart cannot make much of the proclamation of the kingdom. Applying pressure to the closed heart is not the right approach; *we must know the difference between pressure and persuasion.*

Neither the reality of the preconditions of the heart nor the rocky soil of our cultural or familial landscape should lead us to simply throw up our hands in resignation. Hope, the very opposite of resignation, is the special disposition of the Christian. By avoiding the interpretation to apply pressure, we can do a great deal to persuade those who appear to be a distance away from the goal.

In the first place, we can depend upon the interior and persistent action of the Holy Spirit. We can recall cases where previously nonpracticing Catholics suddenly started to pray or return to Mass. These experiences prove that in a mysterious way, God works to draw everyone to himself. Before we say or do anything, the Holy Spirit acts upon the interior of the person. The Holy Spirit acts inside the heart (even in the heart's coldness), prompting the will to move towards the good, and enlightening the mind to grasp the true. Jesus is capable of drawing to himself those farthest away; his power is not limited like a governor's, whose laws suddenly become ineffective at the state border. He is not only "granted license" within the Church; his action extends everywhere, including out to the frontiers. As collaborators with the God whose center is everywhere and whose circumference is nowhere, we may intercede for friends and family who do not follow Christ. And we can motivate them as his ambassador, using the conciliatory language of persuasion rather than the harsh tongue of pressurizing speech.

This interior movement of the Holy Spirit must be accompanied and complemented by the exterior persuasion of the evangelizer. The most skillful missionaries know how to motivate and how to persuade; they understand how to make faith attractive. They spend time thinking about how to approach people in language that reaches them in their particular context. Before we take issue with the ostensible flexibility or looseness of this approach, we should remember that Saint Paul himself remarked that he had "become all things to all men, to save at least some" (1 Cor 9:22). To shapeshift in the way of Saint Paul does not mean to compromise the gospel. Think back to Martin Buber's analysis of the role of the educator. The teacher who meets a roomful of apathetic teenagers falls short if he asks them to merely repeat principles out of a textbook, even if done with admirable clarity. He must come to "rest on the surface of the spirits" in the classroom, must seek to discover the curiosities that lie underneath the indifferent exteriors of his students. Then, the teacher may find an enlivening method. If he makes application to relevant social scenarios, if he speaks in a relatable way, he is enhancing the material rather than compromising it. Just as the teacher is responsible for meeting students at their respective starting points, the missionary is responsible for presenting the faith in an appealing, creative, and comprehensible manner.

It is not all about strategy however: the teacher who truly inspires, who brings the material alive, reaches the students not only from cleverness but also from the *communication of his own passion*. Even the most talented teacher will struggle to convince students to engage if he does not see the value of what he teaches. His unfaked ardor is the factor that authenticates his work. Connection must be twofold: connection to people *and* connection to the source. One who "becomes all things to all men" is influential and resourceful as long as he believes in and express sincere conviction in what he shares.

In evangelization, the marker of authenticity is joy—a fruit of the Spirit. Joy lies at the root of attractive evangelization, creating this attraction from within rather than adding it on like a kind of cosmetic procedure. In *Evangelii Gaudium*, Pope Francis sketches the countenance of missionary joy: "Christians have the duty to proclaim the Gospel without excluding anyone. Instead of seeming to impose new obligations, they should appear as people who wish to share their joy, who point to a horizon of beauty and who invite others to a delicious banquet. It is not by proselytizing that the Church grows, but by attraction."[1]

To evangelize is to point towards the beautiful that has already been given, to invite to the table prepared in advance by God. As good news, Christianity is inherently luminous, inherently attractive. The Greek word for grace, *charis*, also means "the attractiveness of the beautiful." Luminosity emanates from the light that shines from within—as a light of a bulb, rather than like a spotlight. Through faithful return to dependence on the Holy Spirit, our presentation should come across as positive and luminous. In fact, if it does not, this is not just a sign of an inferior method, but a sign that we are not drawing from the source. If grounded in the action of the Holy Spirit, the presentation of the gospel will shine.

In the Saint John Society, we seek to express positivity and luminosity in all our mission work. This emphasis is present in our light-filled churches, in our joyful missionary style, and in our preaching, which emphasizes Christianity as good news. As described in our unpublished constitution: "We foster a positive proclamation of the Christian faith that shows its intrinsic attractiveness and richness, as well as its relevance for people's lives. We know that this positive proclamation—as is shown

1. EG, 15.

64

by the multitudes that followed Jesus—is always capable of awakening a desire in the human heart."

In short, we present Christianity as positive—*because it is positive*. We present it as relevant because it is relevant, attractive because it is attractive.

The Way of Persuasion: "It Is Easy to Evangelize!"

Remember that Pope Paul VI called Jesus "the greatest evangelizer"; as the greatest evangelizer, Jesus was by definition an expert in the way of persuasion. In his earthly ministry, he questioned and called—take Zacchaeus and Matthew, for instance—and people responded and came. He sat with people, listened to them, and then astounded them with his insight and his promise, as he did with the Samaritan woman. He reached out through the instrument of his exemplary humanity to draw people into the unfathomable riches of his divinity.

The influence of Jesus may be understood objectively as the fruit of God's action, as the achievement of the love of God, but we can still ask, humanly, subjectively, "What made Jesus so persuasive?" Why, in turn, is Christianity so persuasive? Succinctly stated, Christ persuades people to come to him because he gives—he *is*—the deepest response to the questions and the needs of the human heart. He provides satisfaction to the infinite longing of our finite hearts, and he opens us again to the depths of the infinite—a process of growth without cap, an adventure into boundlessness. For if he is the final answer to all our questions, then he is also the question to all our answers; he is the ever-greater God in human flesh, taking us beyond ourselves even as he reaches into what is most central in us! He quenches our thirst with water from a limitless lake, rather than from an exhaustible jug: he always has more to give.

Fr. Iván Pertiné, the general director of the Saint John Society, once casually remarked to our community, "It is easy to evangelize!" Impulsively, a missionary in formation questioned him: "What do you mean? It seems like it is difficult to evangelize—opposition and resistance are everywhere." Fr. Iván responded confidently, "I understand your point, but what we have to offer is what people long for the most. Therefore, it is easy to evangelize." Christianity fits the human heart as a glove fits the hand. By preaching Christ, we preach what satisfies the deepest human longings; resistance and opposition are seen properly as barriers unequal to the ultimate fulfillment they obstruct.

The Metaphysical Persuasion of
the Real: The Transcendentals

We have outlined the first indications of the importance of drawing people to God both through the intercession that "unleashes" the inner persuasion of the Holy Spirit and through an outward proclamation that inspires the spiritual seeker to move towards faith. The ministry of persuasion has both metaphysical and Christological roots.

The Christian view coincides with a realist metaphysics. The world has a sacramental character; it is a visible manifestation of the invisible: the created comes from the uncreated, the finite from the infinite. This approach invites us to see the world as cosmos and as mystery. We have a metaphysical or philosophical respect for what is real.

In ancient and medieval philosophy, the concept of a *transcendental* refers to that which is common to all being, eventually understood primarily as fourfold: the transcendentals are unity, goodness, truth, and beauty. Everything possesses the transcendentals; the only question is of degree. The transcendentals are each convertible with being, meaning that they each represent an aspect of the same reality: the greater the truth of something, the greater the goodness, and the greater the goodness and truth, the greater the being. The closer something approximates its ideal form, the more it possesses each of these transcendentals in fullness. For instance, the more ferocious, lithe, and alert a particular lion, the more the lion possesses the transcendentals of beauty, truth, goodness, and being, and the more it is truly a lion: the more it *exists*! Each transcendental bespeaks and yields the others. Each is a ray emanating from the same source of light. As Hans Urs von Balthasar writes, "The light of the transcendentals, unity, truth, goodness, and beauty . . . can only shine if this light is undivided."[2] They pertain to everything in the world, and they point to the absolute being, truth, goodness, and beauty of God, who is forever beyond all earthly determinants, even while revealing a likeness to each of them. Since God, who is also known as the Subsistent Being, is infinite, the transcendentals can be many and varied, perhaps even indefinite. Philosophy speaks of the good, true, beautiful, and as the most archetypal or recognizable of the transcendentals. But we could also add others such as order, luminosity, venerability, etc.[3]

2. Balthasar, *Word Made Flesh*, 107.

3. Komar, *Vitalidad Intelectual*, 169.

This created vision of reality allows us to affirm that the human person is capable of contemplating what is real, "feeding" upon the real, and even entering into dialogue with the real. Emiliano Komar says:

> All reality comes from the hands of God, because creation is pre-thought and pre-loved by Him. Accordingly, the things that are real inspire intellectual interest, but at the same time, they stimulate our capacity for love. That is why deeply known things end up being loved, and things really loved end up being well known . . . they share a common root because all being—what there is—that is, the truly existing, includes in itself the actuality that makes it exist, thus reaching our affective capacity, stirring it and stimulating love, and also our cognitive capacity, illuminating it.[4]

Being is inherently attractive; the fullness of being *persuades* us towards deepening communion. Through knowledge, we enter into dialogue with the logic by which God has structured reality. Through our will, we love the inherent goodness that God has placed at the heart of everything. This metaphysical vision leads us to a personalist philosophy: the human person nourishes his deepest powers, intelligence, and will through dialogue with the real, which is grounded in the personal God.

The Supernatural Persuasion of Christianity: Jesus as Way, Truth, and Life

After this brief metaphysical sketch, we can now turn to the Christological foundations of persuasion. If we hold that everything real is good, true, beautiful, and one, how much more does this principle apply to the incarnate Word! Eternally, the person of the Word possesses the fullness of being. In the incarnation, that fullness is manifested in a visible way. He is the visible image of the invisible God (Col 1:15), and in him dwells the fullness of divinity (Col 2:19), etc. He is the truth and speaks to us of the ultimate truth. He is goodness itself; everything he does, he does well. He is the beautiful shepherd who draws the sheep to himself. He is the unified man who is fully aware of his deepest identity. In him, the transcendentals shine and overflow.

Looking now at the declarations of Jesus as the Way, the Truth, and the Life, notice the foundational unity of the triad, akin to the unity of the transcendentals. The Way can be the way only if it is paved by truth; any

---

4. Komar, *Vitalidad Intelectual*, 68.

note of falsity and it would not be *the Way* but something lesser, a way of only questionable promise. The Truth and the Life flourish together; consider how receiving a profound truth evokes the same renewal of the spiritual life: awe at the reception of something greater than oneself. And then the abundant Life of Christ leads one to follow along the Way that he calls upon his disciples to follow; in the measure that life in Christ renews, it leads to following his path of love: his is the Life that imparts righteousness. This intrinsic unity also bears direct correspondence to the transcendentals themselves, as well as to Christianity as a religion, a notion Peter Kreeft unfolds in *Catholics and Protestants: What Can We Learn From Each Other?* He writes:

> Jesus said: "I am the way, and the truth, and the life, no man comes to the Father, but by me" (Jn 14:5–6). The way, the truth, and the life are the three things we all need the most, and therefore desire the most, deep down. The way is goodness; the truth is truth, and the life is spiritual life, beauty, bliss, and joy. Goodness, truth, and beauty are the three essential foods of the soul.
>
> They are also the object of the soul's three distinctively human powers (the will, the mind, and the heart). Plato called these three powers of the soul, the spirited part, the reason, and the appetites.
>
> They correspond to the three dimensions in every religion: code, creed, and cult; or works, words and worship. There are dimensions of a single reality, like the three dimensions of space. It is a very same reality that Christians obey in their morality, confess in their theology, and participate in their liturgy. That "very same reality" is Christ. These three dimensions are not three parts; you can separate parts in reality as well as in thought; you can separate dimensions only in thought.[5]

The person of Christ, and consequently the Christianity through which he meets us, is the food that nourishes the soul. The nourishment takes place through a code that summarizes the goodness of Christian morality, a creed that expresses the truths of divine revelation, and the cult or form of worship that reveals the surpassing beauty of Christ. Missionaries gesture, teach, and encourage so that people may follow, see, and draw strength according to Christ's gift. As missionaries, we return to this central affirmation: the fullness of being—the object of every human search—is present in him and mediated by him! From this vantage point, we can see how one might say, without irony: "It is easy to evangelize."

5. Kreeft, *Catholics and Protestants*, 161.

The Persuasion of Jesus in the Transfiguration

Let's now examine Jesus's transfiguration *in light of the unified light* of the transcendentals. Read Luke 9:28–36 before going on. Keep an eye out for how Christ's attraction flows through the transcendentals. Beginning from the transfiguration account, we can then observe how the three transcendentals are like three avenues, starting from different cardinal directions, that converge at the center of the city; they are the three avenues that walk the seeker into the heart of the faith.

The Life (the Heart, the Beautiful, and the Liturgy): In the transfiguration episode, Peter, James, and John are *awakened*—in both senses of the word—by the truth, beauty, and goodness of Christ. We should observe their process of discovery closely, for the experience of the disciples in the Gospels is archetypal for all those coming to knowledge of Christ.

Emerging from sleep, the disciples immediately encounter the beauty of Christ. The first thing Peter and the other two see is the "glory" of Christ, beholding him as he appears in the revelatory form that anticipates the resurrection. Are they initially awakened by his dazzling transfiguration, in the way that flashing lights might suddenly stir a sleeper to alertness? Or do they first wake up and then catch sight of his glory, like someone napping at the park emerging from their fog to a nearby conversation gradually becoming audible? The passage does not make this clear, but we must suppose that the sight of the glory of the Lord sharpens them into a state of excitement and uncommon attention. They must have been entirely absorbed in the sight before them, beside themselves in the thrill of what they were witnessing.

This state of absorption and transportation, a kind of ecstasy (literally, being taken out of oneself), is the effect of an experience of beauty. Saint Thomas Aquinas conceives of beauty as the *splendor* of truth and goodness. We could say as well that beauty is that dimension of the good and the true that shines and draws us in. Again, we see the unity of the transcendentals, the manner in which they reveal one another as inseparable facets of being. The beautiful may also be defined even less technically—according to our experience of it. The beautiful is "something that pleases when it is seen." When beauty is perceived, it brings pleasure to the soul. Christ is the beautiful par excellence, drawing and satisfying the soul.

The beauty of Christ is always present, but we are not always aware. Sometimes we get a glimpse of Christ in the mode of the transfiguration, as a special epiphany in prayer, in the liturgy, or in our neighbor: when we encounter Christ like this, it is as if we realize that all along we have not seen, at least not clearly. Our experience of personal relationships provides an analogy to the nature of this spiritual breakthrough. Sometimes we find that we have been in the same community as someone for a year or more and yet hardly scratched the surface with them, either out of indifference or lack of opportunity. Then, through a chance event, we forge a connection, and we come to realize how much there is to this person whom we had previously passed by without second thought. Looking back standing within the atmosphere of our present closeness, we can hardly believe we were ever so aloof. This is only a dim analogy for the consciousness that begins to dawn on us as we stir from our drowsiness and behold Christ in his splendor: how, we ask, had we gone so long without being overwhelmed by the marvelous depths of his divinity?

As evangelizers, though we cannot produce such an encounter for someone else, we should place ourselves at the service of beauty—expressing the beauty of God through music, art, and decor. Above all, we can find the beauty of Christ in the liturgy. Pope Francis speaks of the way of beauty as the path to approach the heart, a path that invariably surfaces the other transcendentals:

> Every form of catechesis would do well to attend to the "way of beauty" (*via pulchritudinis*). Proclaiming Christ means showing that to believe in and to follow him is not only something right and true, but also something beautiful, capable of filling life with new splendor and profound joy, even in the midst of difficulties. Every expression of true beauty can thus be acknowledged as a path leading to an encounter with the Lord Jesus. This has nothing to do with fostering an aesthetic relativism which would downplay the inseparable bond between truth, goodness, and beauty, but rather a renewed esteem for beauty as a means of touching the human heart and enabling the truth and goodness of the Risen Christ to radiate within it. If, as Saint Augustine says, we love only that which is beautiful, then the incarnate Son, as the revelation of infinite beauty, is supremely lovable and draws us to himself with bonds of love.[6]

The soul cannot live without beauty; even the good and the true lose their vibrancy and positively shrivel if beauty has been excluded. We instinctively seek beauty wherever we go—if not in the Church, then in the world. But in the world, we stumble over a beauty that entices and

6. EG, 167.

ultimately enslaves, a beauty that evaporates if it does not curdle, a beauty that disappoints in its ephemerality. Let us have the missionary courage to present beauty in the form of the Christian inheritance, which includes sacred art and the liturgy, as well as the humble beauty of a life devoted to Christ and in service to our neighbor.

The Truth (the Mind, the True, and the Creed): At the mountaintop before Peter, James, and John, Jesus reveals the truth of who God is and the truth of the plan of salvation. The transfiguration scene—and likewise the encounter with the truth of our faith—grants access and confidence where obstructions and doubts had previously reigned; if the luminosity of the beautiful is the warm light that draws towards itself, then the luminosity of the truth is the light that penetrates the darkness and discloses the real! *For many disciples, this is the light along the path that soothes fear and provides the courage to continue.*

The transfiguration scene reveals two key dimensions of Christian truth. First, the passage is an epiphany of God's identity, both the Trinitarian nature of God and the divinity of Christ. Jesus speaks, and the Father confirms him from above, proclaiming him as "*my beloved Son*": these are also the words the Father pronounces over Jesus at his baptism at the Jordan River; now, at the transfiguration, the Father confirms Jesus as his Son in the course of his ministry, with the suffering and death Jesus has just announced to his disciples looming around the corner.

Second, this reveals the depth and direction of God's redemptive plan. Jesus talks with Moses and Elijah, who represent the Law and the Prophets of the Old Testament, respectively. His conversation thereby represents a continuation of the dialogue between God and God's people, demonstrating that his life carries on the Father's plan for the salvation of humanity and the renewal of all of creation. He speaks to Moses and Elijah precisely of the plan's linchpin—his "exodus," by which he indicates the paschal mystery: his suffering, death, and resurrection. Through his exodus, he liberates the world!

These mountaintop revelations address Peter in a particular way. Just before being led up the mountain, Peter had rejected the notion of the passion, and Jesus had rebuked him. But now he begins to grasp the fullness of the truth—the necessary implications of Jesus's mission as the Son of God. Peter's reservations are addressed as he "listen[s] to him," just as the Father instructs him to do. He can now place his initial feeling at the prospect of

Jesus's death in the perspective of Jesus's sonship, in the perspective of the good plan of the Father. Peter has been given insight!

Similarly, for those on the way, the intellectual path dispels resistance, leading people towards a new horizon. To facilitate this perspective, we can turn to the Catholic Creed, the appropriate launching point for students of Catholicism. The creed presents the articles of our belief; it is the "summary of the faith in a page," as Abbott Jeremy Driscoll of Mount Angel Abbey says. Now, this page must be read like a table of contents, that is, as an indication of the full text. The sustained exploration of the articles of the creed, in one form or another, becomes the substance of the Catholic intellectual life. There are those who lean heavily on the transcendental of truth, who "read themselves into the faith," gaining through study an awareness of the coherence, richness, and love of God's plan of salvation. Much like Peter, who experienced a direct vision of God's plan for Jesus, this vision may provide the perspective they need in order to surrender themselves more fully in faith.

Following the passion, Peter reminds his community of the significance of the intellectual dimension: "Always be ready to give an explanation to anyone who asks you for a reason for your hope, but do it with gentleness and reverence" (1 Pet 3:15–16). Peter implies that we have reasons for our hope. Indeed, we do. We can supply rational foundations for the existence of God, the historicity of New Testament events, the compatibility of faith and science, etc. When taken together, the various sources of evidence for the truth of Christianity represent what John Henry Newman calls the convergence of probabilities. These sources point to the reality of Christ from different angles, possessing a kind of cumulative effect when compiled, like adding the testimony of witness after witness to a certain event. Not one should be seen in isolation as an open-and-shut case, as the final word on Christianity, but each informs and strengthens the greater composite picture of the reasonableness of the faith.

Peter anticipates the tendency we have, when justifying our faith, to grow combative, to explain ourselves defensively or scornfully, and he wisely recognizes that this approach is counterproductive; to preach with hostility would be to preach the gospel while lacking the spirit of the gospel. If we listen to Peter's instruction to always be prepared to explain our faith, we should take his second clause just as seriously, sharing our reasons "with gentleness and reverence." Saint Francis de Sales stands as his veritable interpreter through the aphorism "a spoonful of honey attracts more flies than a barrelful of vinegar." Negative energy merely creates more negative energy, not disciples. Moreover, when we speak positively, we honor the intellectual quest of the person we meet. We can invite them to continue their quest through books, videos, and resources from modern-day evangelists like Bishop Robert Barron, and, where appropriate, through intercourse with the great minds of our tradition like Newman, Aquinas, Augustine, and Bonaventure.

The Way (the Will, the Good, and the Code of Christ): In the transfiguration scene, Peter exclaims, "Master, it is good that we are here!" The beauty, truth, and goodness of the transfigured Christ satisfy the deepest desires of the three disciples. Naturally, the disciples want to remain in this state of satiety. Their inner joy is completed by the experience of Christ's goodness, experienced in fullness at Tabor. This goodness is experienced on three levels.

First, the disciples experience the goodness of Jesus himself. The Father tells Jesus that he is his chosen Son. He is the Father's beloved from all eternity. Upon Jesus, the Father pours out the infinite love of the Holy Spirit. Jesus knows he is loved. He is aware of his intrinsic goodness. And for that reason, he becomes the pearl of great price, the hidden treasure that satisfies our hearts.

Second, they experience the goodness of Trinitarian communion. They are in the presence of a Trinitarian epiphany. They enter the stream of love that is constantly being exchanged between the three divine persons. The whole Trinity, the very icon of the infinite outpouring of love, is present before the disciples! On the mountaintop, the Holy Spirit and the Father reveal themselves in communion with Jesus for their sake.

Third, they experience the goodness of Christ's teachings. The Father confers authority on his Son by saying to the disciples, "Listen to him." The Father effectively communicates, "He will teach you the art of living. He will give you a code of life that liberates you and enables you to thrive. He will tell you what is most essential." The moral code of Christianity emerges from the heart of the Trinity and leads to the flourishing of the human person. Moral rules are not arbitrary impositions; they do not oppress but elevate. Moral rules teach us to live as the divine persons live, in full communion and mutual self-donation. The words and deeds of Jesus are good because they allow us to walk that path. The principal moral teachings of the Old Testament (the Ten Commandments) and the teachings of Jesus in the New (the Beatitudes) are the applied precepts that teach us how to enter into the stream of divine love.

As evangelizers, we must appeal to the will, must ultimately drop down from the clouds of the intellect and emphasize the power of a life lived in concrete practices of love. Our will gains strength and inspiration from Christ's model of loving self-sacrifice. If, generalizing broadly, the "head types" tend to read and reason their way into the faith, then predominantly relational people often come to faith through friendship with a Christian or connection with a Christian community. The testimony of a Christian, the light of Christian morality, the experience of support or belonging, and the works of mercy can each serve as an entrance door.

These entrance doors, theologically considered, are carved by the communion demonstrated and advanced on Mt. Tabor. Testimony, Christian charity, and the works of mercy point back to the fullness of divine love manifested at the transfiguration; likewise, the transfiguration points forward to these fruits of the Spirit. The transfiguration is an experience generative of community: the three apostles are drawn into the divine community of love of the Holy Trinity, as well as the community of fidelity constituted by Jesus, Moses, and Elijah. Here, we come to the final transcendental, which we have spoken little of thus far: the transcendental of unity. When beauty, truth, and goodness converge, they form their consummate expression in the Christian community: the mystery that each Christian reveals in fragments is carried whole and entire by the body of Christ.

Peter, James, and John directly experience the goodness, truth, and beauty of Jesus on Mount Tabor. Peter's words convey the effect of the reception of this unified light: "Rabbi, it is good that we are here! Let us make three tents: one for you, one for Moses, and one for Elijah." For good reason, the disciples want to stay. When they come down from the mountain, whether they share the experience with others explicitly or not (in the Gospels of Mark and John, Jesus tells them not to), they are fortified for evangelization. They are prepared for the radiant ministry of attraction, which only shines if it shines out from within—and only persuades if suffused with the power from on high.

Application

Evangelization by attraction implies developing disciples capable of friendship, cultivating communities of welcome, and presenting Christianity as a path of liberation.

Consider these approaches to participation in the work of persuasion:

1. Pray to the Holy Spirit that he may persuade people from within. Before you meet with someone about their faith, ask for the coming of the Holy Spirit to intervene and open their heart. As we say in the Saint John Society, "Before bringing God before people, bring people before God."

2. Make use of the three transcendentals to awaken curiosity:

   - Develop habits of sharing your intellectual life: If you read a good book, recommend it to a friend—and offer to talk about the book with your friend as they are reading it. Send inspiring articles to a group of your contacts to stimulate conversation.

   - Be generous with your time. Let the people making their way towards the Church know that you are available in friendship, and that your friendship does not depend on their "status" or progress in Christ.

   - Share the places, experiences, and occasions that fill you with a sense of the beauty of the Church. Invite to an Easter Vigil Mass; share information on those places that fill you with peace.

3. Discover your personal style of evangelization. Are you predominantly truth-, beauty-, or goodness-oriented? Whatever you determine your strength to be, season your approach with the salt of the other transcendentals, but don't be afraid to give of the gift that you possess most abundantly!

CHAPTER SIX

Prayer: The Foundation of Missionary Life

OUR NEXT P IS the foundation of the missionary life. This is the prayer of the missionary, which stimulates, fuels, and directs mission. For a great and encouraging primer on prayer, we recommend *Thirsting for Prayer* by Fr. Jacques Philippe. Here, we limit ourselves to consideration of three modes of prayer specific to evangelization: prayer of the missionary, prayer for the mission, and prayer with the missionaries.

Prayer of the Missionary

Evangelization is like an iceberg: the tip is the visible public life; beneath lies the holiness of the missionary. Only if we are in relationship with Christ can we speak about him with naturality and conviction. Saint Pope John Paul II, who was both a great missionary and a great mystic, reminds us of the missionary's need for communion:

> An essential characteristic of missionary spirituality is intimate communion with Christ. . . . The call to mission derives from the call to holiness. A missionary is really such only if he commits himself to the way of holiness: holiness must be called a fundamental presupposition and an irreplaceable condition for everyone in fulfilling the mission of salvation of the Church. The universal call to holiness is closely linked to the universal call to mission . . . unless the missionary is a contemplative, he cannot proclaim Christ in a credible way.[1]

Our model evangelizer made this interconnection between mission and prayer especially apparent. Jesus spent great periods of his public life in

1. RM, §§88–91.

prayer. Despite his constant activity, he always made time to pray, especially before sunrise and at the end of the day. He not only set prayer time apart, but he also weaved together mission and prayer, jumping from prayer to mission and from mission to prayer. Before he raised Lazarus, for instance, Jesus prayed aloud in gratitude to the Father (John 11:41).

In the first chapter of Mark's Gospel, Jesus and his disciples have an illuminating exchange. He has gone up to the mountain to pray. Peter and others with him come to Jesus and say, "Everyone is looking for you." Jesus responds, "Let us go on to the nearby villages that I may preach there also. For this purpose have I come" (Mark 1:36–38). We can see Jesus's reply to Peter as a response based on two conversations: both his conversation with the Father in prayer and his conversation with Peter. In dialogue with the Father, he communicated about the purpose for which he came, about the activity he would undertake to fulfill his task. Jesus's prayer intensified his relationship with his mission. The great evangelizers of the Church have followed suit: Saint Paul, Saint Patrick, Saint Dominic, Saint Francis Xavier, and Saint Frances Cabrini were each marked by a deep life of prayer.

In order to proclaim, we must be holy! To be holy is not to be flawless nor to be free of all wounds; it is not that you must wait for confirmation of spiritual perfection in order to proclaim Christ. Rather, and simply, the defining element is a deep desire and our love for God. All the people mentioned above, despite their wide-ranging dispositions and circumstances, have in common a profound anointing from above and a deep love, the love that becomes the leaven of the world. Only the saints will transform the world. Living a life of holiness, being on fire with the love for Jesus, is the most important factor in the New Evangelization.

In the Saint John Society, we are inspired to imitate the public life of Jesus. Of course, this central focus does not imply that we bypass the contemplative or "hidden life." With this missionary balance in mind, we would like to reflect on Jesus's appointment of the apostles in Mark 3:14: "He appointed twelve [whom he also named apostles] that they might be with him and he might send them forth to preach." Jesus calls the apostles to two primary actions: to be with him and to go out. Here again we return to the core New Testament dynamic—the "coming and the going."

The missionary's first task is to be with Jesus. The apostles are sent forth only from the secure base of their intimacy with him. What does "being with him" mean for us? It includes all the different, integrated levels that strengthen our faith: a personal life of prayer, community life, fruitful access to the sacraments, and the study of our faith. If we are not first spending time with Jesus, then we cannot be sent to preach with power.

This first dimension, the prayer of the missionary, begins with developing a prayer life that keeps you engrafted to the vine (John 15:4). Prayer life allows you to:

1. Develop a life of holiness that radiates the presence of Christ—in Saint Paul's words, a life that emits "the fragrance of Christ."

2. Nurture the flame of love. As John Paul II reminds us, "Missionary spirituality is also marked by apostolic charity. . . . Those who have the missionary spirit feel Christ's burning love for souls."[2]

3. Follow the inspirations of the Holy Spirit to respond to the needs of each person.

4. Keep your love for the Lord alive.

Archbishop Francis Xavier Nguyen Van Thuan presents a striking example of the priority of prayer with respect to mission. As bishop of Saigon, he was captured during the Vietnam War by North Vietnamese troops in 1975. He spent thirteen years in Communist prisons, nine of those in solitary confinement. All the while, he continued to pray and sneak messages of hope out to his people. He later said that in prison he learned to trust God with total self-abandonment. He reports that early on during his time in prison, while he was worried about how his archdiocese was faring in his absence, he heard a voice give him this message:

> You must distinguish between God and the works of God. Everything you have done and desire to continue doing—pastoral visits, formation of seminarians, of men and women religious, of the laity, of the youth, construction of schools, *foyers* for students, missions for the evangelization of non-Christians—all of these are excellent works. These are God's works, but *they* are not God.[3]

Thuan said that a new peace and light entered his heart upon receiving this epiphany. The duty of each Christian is to choose God first! Then God

2. RM, §89.

3. Thuan, *Testimony of Hope*, 42.

will direct the works he wishes each of us to accomplish. To choose God first is to make the choice to start with prayer—and to follow the paths that God opens from within this space. As much as prayer is a necessary precondition for mission, it is not simply an instrument for mission; rather, it represents our fundamental and all-important choice for God above all else.

Prayer for the Mission

Prayer for the mission is the second dimension of missionary prayer. As we saw, persuasion contains both interior and exterior aspects, with the interior aspect generating the exterior. Interior persuasion is the action of the Holy Spirit in the heart of each person, leading that person either to accept the gospel for the first time or to go deeper into his or her life of faith. As missionaries, we are collaborators rather than creators; we collaborate with the sanctifying action of God. It is not that God is helping *us* lead someone to faith. Rather, we are helping with God's action. He is much more invested than we are!

In our collaborative endeavor, intercessory prayer becomes a key element of the mission. The missionary spends a great share of his or her prayer life praying for others. The catechism speaks of this practice of "looking out" for others in prayer, in which we detach from our own needs to place those for whom we intercede before God's mercy: "In intercession, he who prays looks 'not only to his own interests, but also to the interests of others.'"[4] Our intercessory prayer stems from our concern for others; in this way, it emerges from the dynamic of our own life, just as personal petitionary prayer begins with our present personal needs in the context of our discipleship.

Intercessory prayer is also a deep part of the tradition of the Church, both in the Scriptures and in the saints. In the Old Testament, Abraham intercedes for the good men numbered among the wicked in Sodom, veritably twisting God's arm in an effort to save them (Gen 18:22–23). Moses intercedes for the people of Israel following their betrayal through worship of the golden calf (Exod 32:11–13). He prays for them even in their guilt. Famously, he also prays continually with his arms raised for Joshua and his army while they are fighting against Amalek (Exod 17:8–16). While his arms are raised, Israel has the better of the fight. When his arms fall, the battle turns. Aaron and Hur physically support Moses's hands, one

4. CCC, §2635.

man on either side, all the way until sunset, and the victory is won. These two alongside Moses complete the image of intercession in the Church, what we might call its communal fortification: the authentic picture of intercession is not simply prayer for one person on behalf of another but fervent prayer—even tireless prayer—supported with equal selflessness by those who share in the mission.

Abraham and Moses, along with all other intercessors from the Bible, prefigure Jesus in his priestly role. Jesus is the true mediator and intercessor between us and the Father. He shows us his intercessory heart in the Scriptures. Through the whole of chapter 17 in John's Gospel, in his high priestly prayer, Jesus brings to the Father the needs of both his present and future disciples. He bids the Father to watch over them and protect them from the evil one, to consecrate them in the truth, and to establish unity between disciples as well as with the Father and the Son. In Luke, Jesus tells Peter that he has already prayed for him that his faith would remain strong, so that he can build up the disciples: "I have prayed that your own faith may not fail; and once you have turned back, you must strengthen your brothers" (Luke 22:32). Coming as this does right before Jesus's prediction of Peter's denial of Jesus, the prayer evinces the power of God to work even in faltering hearts.

Luke also gives us a beautiful priestly image of the ascension of Jesus. As Jesus ascends, he blesses his disciples: "He led them [out] as far as Bethany, raised his hands, and blessed them. As he blessed them, he parted from them and was taken up to heaven" (24:50). The word *blessing* (benediction) comes from the union of two Latin words: *bene* (good) and *dictio* (to say, to wish). To bless means to wish what is good for another person. When Jesus blesses, he does so with the power to remain with those he blesses even in his parting. His hands remain stretched out over the world. He effectively says to the disciples, "I have your back. I will pray for all of you, and I will pray for the mission I have imparted to you."

Jesus's ascension does not make him remote; rather, he ascends to support and guide us continually from the seat of his communion with the Father. As Pope Benedict XVI writes in *Jesus of Nazareth: Holy Week*, "[As the Ascended Lord], he is no longer in one particular place in the world as he had been before the 'Ascension': now, through his power over space, he is present and accessible to all—throughout history and in every place."[5] From this position, Jesus advocates for us and for our needs to the Father.

5. Benedict XVI, *Jesus of Nazareth*, 284.

In Rom 8, wherein Saint Paul affirms the love and providence of God for his chosen ones, Paul invokes the promise of the intercession of the ascended Jesus at the right hand of the Father. Paul says, "Who will condemn? It is Christ [Jesus] who died, rather, was raised, who also is at the right hand of God, who indeed intercedes for us" (Rom 8:34). The Letter to the Hebrews enhances this vision from Romans, presenting Jesus as the high priest who lives before the Father to intercede for us *eternally*: "He [Jesus] is always able to save those who approach God through him, since he lives forever to make intercession for them" (Heb 7:25).

Knowledge of the intercession of Jesus should be ingrained in the soul of a missionary. We must return to the truth that our intercession does not just stand on its own but joins the perpetual intercession of Jesus. When we pray for someone, it is not as if we call Jesus *to us* to ask him to assist in their conversion. Rather, we walk *to Jesus*, where we join in his ongoing intercession for this person. We are not alone when we go out on a new mission. We are not even first. And when we encounter difficulty, when we meet resistance, misunderstanding, or rejection from those for whom we intercede, we are following along his way of the cross. He is no less present and active at these times than when the mission hums.

The saints lend the testimony of their lives to the scriptural tradition regarding intercession. In their intercessory zeal, they show us how grace leads us to enfold more and more people within our thoughts and prayers; the great intercessors reflect the universal heart of Jesus. Although she was not an active missionary, Saint Thérèse of Lisieux is one of the two patrons of the missions of the Church, along with Saint Francis Xavier. Without leaving the convent, she demonstrated a missionary charism in her vocation to pray for missionaries, especially for priests. Even before entering the convent at Carmel, she discovered the power of intercession. As an adolescent, she prayed fervently for the conversion of the famous condemned murderer Pranzini, whom she read about in the newspaper. With the date of his execution approaching, she prayed that Pranzini would show just a single sign of repentance before his last breath. In the last moments of his life, Pranzini mounted the scaffold, turned fully around to the chaplain on hand, and asked for a crucifix, which he then kissed. When Therese read the account in the paper the next day, she was moved to tears, overjoyed with the conviction that her prayer was granted.

Saint Monica, the mother of Saint Augustine, is another classic hero of intercession. Her prayers led not only her son Augustine into faith but her entire family, including her unruly husband Patricius, who asked to be baptized a year before his death. Monica, like many mothers, was unable to be at peace until her family was too. She prayed restlessly for Augustine's conversion until he turned to Christ. She counseled with bishops about his religious wanderings, she brought her prayers to the shrines of martyrs, and she implored Augustine to surrender to God and lead a moral life. In *The Confessions*, although Augustine writes looking back with gratitude, we can still detect his frustration and annoyance while Monica pushed relentlessly for his conversion. When he left for Rome from North Africa, he had to trick Monica by taking her to the shrine of Saint Cyprian and leaving her to pray through the night, and then stealing off to board a ship. Undisturbed in her intention, Monica later followed Augustine across the Mediterranean, joining him in Milan, where she listened closely to the homilies of Saint Ambrose and encouraged her son as he progressively opened his ear to the teachings of the great bishop of Milan.

Monica's heroic merit was her perseverance. She suffered with Augustine, both before he understood the cause of his own suffering and as he became aware of his spiritual condition. She pleaded with him in the midst of his rejection and coldness. When she passed away, at a point at which Augustine had at last been baptized and determined to dedicate his life to God, she told her son that she was ready to depart, peacefully convinced that her work on earth was done. Augustine gives his mother her due for her selfless labor of prayer, seeing her as God's instrument:

> You [God] sent down your help from above and rescued my soul from the depths of this darkness because my mother, your faithful servant, wept to you for me, shedding more tears for my spiritual death than other mothers shed for the bodily death of a son. . . . You heard her and did not despise the tears which streamed down and watered the place where she bowed her head in prayer.[6]

In her steadfastness and her selflessness, Monica is a model of intercession. Like Monica, we contend with the fear that our prayers go unanswered when circumstances do not shift. We may even perceive a growing gulf between our intentions for reconciliation with God and the life trajectory of those for whom we pray. Let us trust that God will send people to strengthen us, as many holy counselors did for Monica. But whether we sense the impact of our prayers while on earth or not, we can trust that our prayers are heard, and that they are efficacious—even if mysteriously so. We can remember as

---

6. Augustine, *Conf.* 3.11.

well that in interceding for others, we are not only doing God's will but *doing as the Son of God does* at the right hand of the Father.

Finally, as we reflect on the prayer for the mission, we can keep in mind our brothers and sisters in Christ. We are right to think initially of those who do not presently believe (as we imitate Monica and Saint Thérèse), but our prayer should also include those who have already accepted the gospel. As we saw, Jesus prays for Peter in Luke 22, and he prays for all his disciples present and future in John 17. Saint Paul mirrors his master. He shares with Timothy that he prays for him "day and night" (2 Tim 1:3). In Ephesians, he prays that his disciples may believe more deeply in the love of God, so that they may come to "know the love of Christ that surpasses knowledge . . . [and] be filled with all the fullness of God" (Eph 3:14–19). We must remember to dedicate part of our intercessory prayer to those who believe, asking for their growth, protection, and anointing. No one of us is unshakeable: we all carry our fragilities and need to be uplifted. And all of us can be led deeper into knowledge of and love for Christ.

Prayer with the Missionaries

The third dimension of missionary prayer is prayer *with* other missionaries. Missionaries can be tempted and can face desolation. They must pray together to remain strong: remember that Moses would not have been able to keep his arms aloft without Aaron and Hur supporting him. Common prayers specific to the mission can often be especially powerful. In Acts 4:29–31, the initial Christian community prays for an increase in boldness in proclamation. As they prayed, the Holy Spirit came, the house shook, and they received the boldness for which they had asked. Imagine those disciples after their prayer: their joy at being filled with the Holy Spirit, and their shared conviction, renewed through an overpowering anointing, almost like a second Pentecost. As missionaries we need ongoing Pentecosts, moments when the community is filled as one with the Holy Spirit. We must pray together to receive these gifts.

In the Saint John Society, one of the central ways in which we come to "be with him" is to pray with the other missionaries. In our apostolates, every week we have sessions of spontaneous common prayer. Before someone goes out on mission, we do a sending prayer. Before we give a talk, we ask for the prayer of another missionary. When we find ourselves in moments of temptation or struggle, we ask others to pray for us. In this manner, we experience the intercession of our friends who join us in our mission.

We also foster prayer in common with our collaborators in mission. We pray in our meetings. We pray together during retreats. One of the most powerful ways of praying with others is to do prayer campaigns for specific intentions or events. Before a Holy Spirit retreat, we ask people outside of the retreat group to participate in a rosary chain or another form of intercessory prayer. If we have a specific intention, we all fast and pray for that intention. Like the first Christians, we are renewed by the anointing of the Holy Spirit as we pray together. We experience that Christ is with us and among us.

Missionary Prayer

One of the missionary traditions in the Saint John Society is to pray the previously unpublished Missionary Prayer prior to going on home visits. Before we head out two by two to visit homes and speak to people about Jesus, we say the Missionary Prayer together before the Blessed Sacrament. The prayer was written by a Spanish La Salle brother. It expresses the feelings that often come up when we evangelize, reminds us that God is with us as we sow the seed of his Word, and returns us to the recognition that we are his instruments.

Lord, when you send us forth to sow, our hands overflow with riches.

Your word fills us with joy when we scatter it upon open ground.

Lord, when you send us forth to sow, we feel poverty in our souls.

We spread the seed that you have given us and wait
uncertainly for the harvest.

And to us, this uncertain sowing seems to be a waste of time,
and it seems to us that there is little seed for the immensity of our fields.

And we are taken aback by the disproportion of your command and our
strength, but faith lets us understand that you are at our side in this task.

And we go on sowing, through the night and the morning fog, we poor
prophets, trusting that you are using us as your humble tools.

Glory to you, Good Father, who gave us your Word, the true seed, and
by the grace of the Holy Spirit, sow it in the Church through us.

Application: Practical Ideas to Incorporate Prayer into Mission

- Have a prayer list in your Bible: keep a list of names in your Bible as a reminder to pray for others. The list can include your family, people you mentor, people you know who are away from God, your priest(s), etc. You can pray for these people as you pray the rosary or as you do eucharistic adoration. Renew the list periodically.

- Don't give up praying for those who are away from the faith. Remember the example of Monica!

- Shower evangelization events with prayer: Pray before, during, and after any apostolic event. Pray that the Holy Spirit may anoint that event. Pray for those who are leading. Pray for those who are attending. After the event, pray that the seeds sown may grow.

- Learn to fast and offer your sufferings for the conversion of others. As Jesus indicated in Matt 17:16–21, a special strength of healing lies in prayer in fasting.

- Pray to the guardian angel of the person to whom you are planning to speak about God. In our door-to-door evangelization in our mission to rural areas, as we knock on the door of the house, we pray that the guardian angels of those living there may assist us in our missionary endeavor.

- Pray along with the liturgy and the liturgical seasons. In the Church, we follow the maxim *lex orandi, lex credendi*, which means, as we pray, so we believe. Prayer directs the action! The Church teaches us to pray for others: in the prayers of the faithful at Mass, we pray for the world, for those who lead, and for all those who suffer. During certain special days, we pray for specific intentions: for peace on January 1, for the legal protection of the unborn on January 22, for priestly vocations on the fourth Sunday of Easter. Praying with the mind and heart of the Church shows us the path to a broader heart in our personal prayer as well.

---------- CHAPTER SEVEN ----------

Power: The Role of Signs and Wonders in the Process of Conversion

Introduction

He said to them, "Go into the whole world and proclaim the gospel to every creature. Whoever believes and is baptized will be saved; whoever does not believe will be condemned.

"These signs will accompany those who believe: in my name they will drive out demons, they will speak new languages. They will pick up serpents with their hands, and if they drink any deadly thing, it will not harm them. They will lay hands on the sick, and they will recover." So then the Lord Jesus, after he spoke to them, was taken up into heaven and took his seat at the right hand of God. But they went forth and preached everywhere, while the Lord worked with them and confirmed the word through accompanying signs. (Mark 16:15–18)

WE NOW MOVE ON to the next *p*: power—by which we mean evangelization by the power of the Holy Spirit.[1] This is a power that transcends merely human capacities, giving evidence of God's action; it is a power by which the Holy Spirit works mighty deeds that demonstrate God's love.

The Scriptures offer the best articulation of the relationship between extraordinary power and the Holy Spirit. In the Acts of the Apostles,

---

1. Our understanding is to be distinguished from power evangelization, a term coined by groups in the Church who seek to evangelize primarily through the manifestation of signs and wonders. Though our notion of power neither denies nor downplays the power of miraculous events and healings to serve as a means of evangelization, we seek to center the proclamation of the gospel and the action of the Holy Spirit before focusing on miraculous events. Such a prioritization, as we argue, stays true to the purpose and significance of signs and wonders as attested by Scripture and as manifested in the early Church.

when Peter describes Jesus's evangelizing work, he closely associates Jesus's anointing with the Holy Spirit and his healings. In his preaching to the gentiles at Caesarea, Peter says, "God anointed Jesus of Nazareth *with the Holy Spirit and power*. He went about doing good and healing all those oppressed by the devil, *for God was with him*" (Acts 10:38; emphasis added). For Peter, power comes along only with the anointing of the Holy Spirit. In Luke's other writing, Acts, Jesus makes the same connection in reference to the disciples' evangelizing work. Before his ascension, Jesus commands the disciples to stay in the city and wait until the power from on high comes (Luke 24:49). Jesus tells the disciples that they will receive this power *when the Holy Spirit comes upon them* (Acts 1:8). The Holy Spirit is the divine bestower of this gift! The New Testament is unequivocal: to receive "power" means to receive the Holy Spirit! The Holy Spirit is the source of the conversions and supernatural manifestations that the disciples witness and facilitate throughout their ministry. This is also the pattern of the New Evangelization: evangelizing with power means to evangelize through the anointing of the Spirit.

The Bible uses many words and phrases to refer to powerful manifestations of the presence of God—most commonly, *mighty deeds, signs and wonders*, and *miracles*. Extraordinary healings, strong deliverances, answers to prayers, and providential events are each particular cases of these broad categories. When we evangelize in the power of the Spirit, these signs of the presence of God accompany the proclamation of the word. This follows according to Jesus's promise: in the Great Commission of Mark 16, Jesus vows to assist the proclamation of the kerygma with signs. As we see play out in the Acts of the Apostles, these signs both help people come to faith and strengthen the faith of the disciples who are doing the evangelizing. Through signs in the ministry of the early Church, we see not only the conversion of nonbelievers but also the increase of the faith of the first missionaries.

We too can anticipate signs and wonders today. However, a great deal depends on our mindset. We could make comparison to the frame of mind of a prospective whale watcher. To sign up to go whale watching, you must have both a special kind of desire and a special kind of expectation. You have to want to see a whale in the first place; the more the prospect excites you, the more apt you are to sign up. Second, you have to expect that a whale will—or, at the very least, could—appear. If lacking this confidence, then you are not going to hand your afternoon over to a potentially frigid trip out on choppy waters. And if you are coerced into signing on by a friend or family member, then you will not exactly be clutching your binoculars.

When it comes to our relationship with God, each of us can sometimes be like the skeptical or reluctant whale watcher. Perhaps we possess desire enough to want to encounter God, but we lack the expectation that he will show up. It is not only the atheist, fixed in the belief that nothing lies beyond this material world, who thinks that God will not show up. Even those of us who believe in the Lord and desire him can subconsciously feel this way. We are all prone to living in practice according to the deistic clockmaker vision of God, as we treat the world around us and our own lives like a self-sustaining, self-sufficient mechanism, left by God to its own devices. We can carry on day by day in this mentality, discounting our chances of an extraordinary encounter with God.

It is the fruit of our missionary experience in the Saint John Society that this vision not only falls short of the fullness of trust in God but also stands as *empirically inaccurate*. We have seen that God can and does enact extraordinary events. In the work of mission, he seeks to aid our human efforts. He is invested in the conversion of hearts today, as he has always been. In the SSJ[2] constitution, we state: "We believe in the signs of the extraordinary work of God. Today we need these signs of the power of the Holy Spirit that makes all things new, in order to renew the marvelous works of the beginnings of the evangelical preaching."[3] We believe that God seeks to outdo the surging wave of secularism with an immense blessing of grace, that he wants to send a strong effusion of his Spirit to create wonder in a world becoming ever more closed to the presence and power of the supernatural, and that for this purpose he wants to support the work of proclamation with signs and wonders.

First and foremost, we believe in extraordinary signs. We place our binoculars to our eyes and lean forward in expectation and readiness to receive God's blessings. Yet, as the name implies, we recognize that such signs are out of the norm: we do not expect the extraordinary to become commonplace. Mark calls them "accompanying signs": they do not take the place of the proclamation but join it. Rather than sufficing as standalone

2. SSJ is the official abbreviation for the Saint John Society—in Spanish, *Sociedad de San Juan*.

3. "Creemos en los signos del obrar extraordinario de Dios. Necesitamos hoy de estos signos del poder extraordinario del Espíritu que renueva todas las cosas, para que se renueven las maravillas obras en los comienzos de la predicación evangélica" (unpubished *Constituciones*, §14).

entities, they orbit the proclamation, the authentic center, like the moon does the earth. These signs work together both with the kerygmatic proclamation and the administration of the sacraments. Proclamation and sacraments constitute the ordinary ways through which God communicates his life to us, as reliable means of grace. But in addition to the steadiness of this "regular" system, extraordinary signs come to assist in our weakness and doubts, revealing the extravagance of God's love.

Second, we read the signs as indications of the renewing power of the Holy Spirit. In the book of Revelation, Jesus says, "Behold, I make all things new" (Rev 21:5). He tells us that he is actively revitalizing the world, which he achieves through the Spirit. Extraordinary signs are one manifestation of Jesus's labor of renewal. As the Spirit fills the cup, the cup overflows. The signs make evident the overflowing presence of the Spirit today, as they also represent the flow of the final age into the present, heralding the ultimate transformation of the world. They anticipate the wholeness and glory of heaven, wherein all tears and suffering will be no more. They show us a taste of God's power to raise life beyond its present level, beyond the groaning that all creation shares in until God enacts the final transformation of the heavens and the earth.

Third, we value signs and wonders for their evangelical telos: just like the proclamation itself, they aim at leading us to faith. As with the first wave of evangelization following the resurrection—the initial proclamation of the apostles—extraordinary signs validate and reinforce the Spirit-filled preaching. They are not a fascinating object to merely stir our curiosity but a marvel to aid our minds in apprehending the power of God. Just as God blessed the first evangelization wave with remarkable momentum, we believe that God wants to bless the New Evangelization in today's world—set as we are in a new apostolic age. God does not ration the gift of the Spirit: we may trust that he will bless our times with signs of his presence.

Foundations of Expectation

We ground our expectancy of the supernatural in the incarnation, in the history of the Church, and in the pastoral experience of the Saint John Society. As people listened to Jesus's words while he walked the earth, they encountered his mysterious strength and came to faith, but they also witnessed powerful deeds that confirmed the proclamation. These witnesses were able to say decisively, "God is acting here and now." As we hear in *Evangelii Nuntiandi*, Christ's proclamation includes ample manifestations of power:

> Christ also carries out this proclamation by innumerable signs, which amaze the crowds and at the same time draw them to Him in order to see Him, listen to Him and allow themselves to be transformed by Him: the sick are cured, water is changed into wine, bread is multiplied, the dead come back to life. . . . He accomplishes His revelation, completing it and confirming it by the entire revelation that He makes of Himself, by words and deeds, by signs and miracles, and more especially by His death, by His resurrection and by the sending of the Spirit of Truth.[4]

These signs and wonders continue throughout the history of the Church; Christ passes the baton to his disciples, and from these first few, the power spreads out. In the Acts of the Apostles and several New Testament epistles, miracles guide multitudes to faith. Take one characteristic account from Acts, Philip's proclamation:

> Thus, Philip went down to [the] city of Samaria and proclaimed the Messiah to them. With one accord, the crowds paid attention to what was said by Philip when they heard it and saw the signs he was doing. For unclean spirits, crying out in a loud voice, came out of many possessed people, and many paralyzed and crippled people were cured. There was great joy in that city. (Acts 8:5–8)

Add to this account some of Peter's remarkable healings, achieved in collaboration with the apostolic community: the healing of the beggar by Peter and John in Acts 3:1–10, the healings of the countless who laid down before his shadow in Acts 5:12–16, and his healing of Aeneas in Acts 9:32–35. Saint Paul manifested this supernatural power as well. In the Letter to the Thessalonians, he even speaks of power plainly as a privileged means of evidence, as he writes: "For our gospel did not come to you in word alone, but also in power and in the holy Spirit and [with] much conviction" (1 Thess 1:5). Hebrews classifies signs, wonders, and power as a form of "testimony" (Heb 2:4). Jesus's closest followers enacted signs and wonders, and they recognized their value as a unique method of validation.

But we must not look for this only in the first generation of Christians, as if the Spirit operates with less intensity in our age than it did in theirs. This would imply what is called a "cessationist" view of the miraculous, which proffers the following argument: Jesus and the apostles enacted a

4. EN, para. 12.

great number of miracles because miracles were necessary in order to establish Christianity in the world, much in the way that a young tree needs to be practically doused with water for the first year of its life in order to survive. But now that Christianity has reached a degree of maturity, so the argument goes, the Church has no need for further miracles: the sacraments and proclamation of the word are sufficient. Miracles might happen—their possibility cannot be excluded entirely—but they are now very rare. Many Catholics implicitly hold this cessationist view, even if they do not advance the theological argument above.

A closer look at the history of the Church reveals this perspective as untenable. Whether we read Saint Augustine's catalog of miracles witnessed in his time in *The City of God* or peruse the biographies of the saints, we notice that where expectation and holiness are present, miracles manifest. If we accept the power of extraordinary signs in the apostolic age, then we must accept their prevalence in subsequent periods as well. God has never ceased working with power. This historical reality follows according to Jesus's promise that faithful people will continue doing his deeds and in fact add greater deeds: "Amen, amen, I say to you, whoever believes in me will do the works that I do, and will do greater ones than these, because I am going to the Father" (John 14:12). Miracles occurred during the time of Jesus. They occurred during the time of the apostles. They occurred during the lives of many saints—and they are happening now.

Communities and persons who are open to the supernatural clear the way for the growth of the kingdom of God. Inasmuch as rationalists, cessationists (material or formal), and skeptics close themselves to supernatural intervention, they turn their back on an important mode of God's action. In fact, the attitude taken towards the supernatural proves to be pivotal in either the flourishing or the languishing of the Church. Bishop Robert Barron links openness to the supernatural in Africa to the growth of Christianity in this region. Moreover, he views the situation of the African Church as a kind of judgment upon Christianity in the West:

> The Church is growing in Africa, not because the people are poorly educated, but because the version of Christianity on offer there is robustly supernatural. As Philip Jenkins and others have shown, African Christianity puts a powerful stress on the miraculous, on eternal life, on the active providence of God, on healing grace, and on the divinity of Jesus. If such an emphasis is naïve, then every Biblical author, every doctor of the Church, and every major theologian until the nineteenth century was

naïve. The reason a supernaturally oriented Christianity grows is that it is congruent with the purposes of the Holy Spirit, and also that it presents something that the world cannot. A commitment to social justice, service of the poor, and environmentalism is obviously praiseworthy, but such a commitment could be made by decent atheists, agnostics, or secularists. Though it follows quite clearly from a supernatural sensibility, it is not, in itself, distinctively Christian. Accordingly, when Christianity collapses into purely this-worldly preoccupations—as it has, sadly, in much of Europe—it rapidly dries up.[5]

Accompanying Signs: Proclamation and Miracles

Pondering the following fundamental questions can bring us to a greater understanding of signs and wonders: 1) What exactly is the nature of the connection between power (signs and wonders, or miracles) and proclamation? 2) What is the ultimate goal of signs and wonders? 3) Which signs and wonders should we expect today? Returning to Mark 16, we can explore each of these questions in the following three sections.

What is the connection between power and proclamation? We notice that signs and wonders emerge in the midst of those who have faith in Jesus. Jesus says, "These signs will accompany *those who believe*," meaning that signs and wonders occur in the context of people and communities of faith. This is why miracles are so often recorded in the lives of the saints. Saint John Henry Newman accordingly calls them the "shadow of holiness." Where we find faith and New Life in Christ, signs and wonders emerge. Newman posits a direct correlation between miracles and faith and prayer:

> As they [miracles] are granted to Evangelists, so are they granted, though in less measure and evidence, to other holy men; and as holy men are not found equally at all times and in all places, therefore miracles are in some places and times more than in others. And since, generally, they are granted to faith and prayer, therefore in a country in which faith and prayer abound, they will be more likely to occur, than where and when faith and prayer are not; so that their occurrence is irregular.[6]

5. Barron, "What Makes the Church Grow?," para. 5.
6. APVS, 280.

Signs and wonders accompany the proclamation of the kerygma. As noted in Mark 16, the Lord "confirmed the word through accompanying signs." The miracles serve to support and reinforce the gospel. This is an all-important concept. We cannot expect signs and wonders without the proclamation of the word; they are "additives to the proclamation." When we proclaim that Jesus is Lord and that he is alive, these signs and wonders may appear as a testimony to this reality.

Once we recognize the power of the Lord, we can be prone to seek relationship with him for the sake of his benefits: this is a constant temptation, a kind of short-circuiting of the spiritual life. Some groups isolate signs and wonders, as if announcing them as the veritable headliner. They organize healing services focused solely on the miraculous. We sometimes see this phenomenon in charismatic groups who have lost their sense of priority. Father Emiliano Tardiff, a missionary priest, tells the story of his invitation to participate in a charismatic congress. When the organizers communicated that he was scheduled to pray for healing at the end of the congress, he asked: "When am I going to preach?" They told him, "No, you will not preach. Preaching is not a part of our program. We would just like you to pray for the sick." Fr. Tardiff replied, "I'm not a miraculous healer: that is not my job description. If I do not evangelize, then I do not pray for the sick. I only pray *after* proclaiming that Jesus has risen! Signs accompany evangelization. We cannot divorce the two!"

In the Gospel narratives, the majority of Jesus's healing miracles are joined with preaching, as portrayed in Matthew and Luke: "He went around all of Galilee, teaching in their synagogues, proclaiming the gospel of the kingdom, and curing every disease and illness among the people" (Matt 4:23); "Great crowds assembled to listen to him and to be cured of their ailments" (Luke 5:15); "A great crowd . . . came to hear him and to be healed of their diseases" (Luke 6:18); "He received them and spoke to them about the kingdom of God, and he healed those who needed to be cured" (Luke 9:11). Jesus preached first, and he then accompanied his preaching by signs and healings. This chronological precedence of proclamation before signs and wonders suggests that miracles have a kind of native soil, that they grow when planted within the soil of persons and communities turned towards the preaching of Jesus and committed to him. "Miraculous" does not equate to random or irrational; miracles are intrinsically ordered to the kingdom of God, and so they tend to spring up along the path of discipleship.

The ideal context for signs and wonders is not only a community of faith but a community that has been instructed about the possibility of signs and wonders. The desire stimulated by instruction creates a channel for God's action. During our Alpha courses, we hold a healing night in which we call for the coming of the Holy Spirit. We do not simply start right away with prayer: we prepare for the healing night by supplying intellectual and spiritual resources. We deliver a presentation about the theology of healing, as well as a spiritual retreat, both of which help the participants gain strength to make their way onto a path of discipleship. The proclamation that participants receive possesses a twofold purpose: it both engenders the necessary faith that facilitates signs and wonders *and* explains the role of signs and wonders in one's personal life of faith and in the Church as a whole. We discover that the signs and wonders that people experience, like healing and deliverance, possess an orientation to their commitment to discipleship. Though the outcomes are genuinely good ends in themselves, they also function as particularly pointed means of clearing obstructions as they move towards conformity to Christ: people may be healed of a pattern of addiction that had made them too ashamed to come to church, or they might be granted a vision that confirms their faith precisely where they had wavered. It is as if the signs and wonders take people by the shoulders, turn them around, and give a healthy push towards Jesus. As people grow in the experience of New Life, they experience interior healing, physical healing, and deliverance from bondage to sin. They gain freedom—the freedom to follow Christ!

The Ordinary and Extraordinary Systems

This interaction between proclamation and power helps us understand the two interrelated systems at work in evangelization. On one side, we have the proclamation of the kerygma, leading to faith and participation in the sacraments. Jesus says to his missionary disciples: "Go into the whole world and proclaim the gospel to every creature. Whoever believes and is baptized will be saved; whoever does not believe will be condemned." Here we see the essential triad of the work of evangelization: first proclamation, then the response of faith, and the sacraments to follow. The triad sets up what could be called the regular, ordinary, or *humble* system of salvation. Without excluding other means, God communicates his life to us through the sacramental system. This system is more subtle in its effects and less attention-grabbing in its means than the miraculous. Nevertheless, it constitutes the essential element of the ongoing work of evangelization!

However, in tandem with this humble, ordinary, or regular system, God in his infinite freedom also authors extraordinary deeds. Signs and wonders are a more overtly evident way in which God communicates his presence. God reserves a certain sovereignty over them; like whale watchers, we cannot be certain that if we go out looking, we will necessarily encounter them. We cannot be assured in advance that signs and wonders will accompany the proclamation; when we celebrate the sacraments, on the other hand, we may be sure of their action, which is why we can enumerate the objective fruits of the Eucharist, penance, confirmation, etc.

God calls all of us to sacramental life. But like the Good Shepherd, he also reaches beyond; he is willing to go outside of his established routes in order to lift us up. Through signs and wonders, he boosts our faith, while also reminding us of the amazing things he accomplishes through the sacraments. Take the miracle of the paralytic: Jesus challenges the crowd who is suspiciously eyeing him, "Which is easier, to say, 'Your sins are forgiven,' or to say, 'Rise and walk'? But that you may know that the Son of Man has authority on earth to forgive sins"—he then said to the paralytic, "Rise, pick up your stretcher, and go home" (Matt 9:5–6). Jesus's miracle of healing engenders belief in the higher spiritual potency: the power to forgive sins. Likewise, though we cannot see what takes place in a soul during absolution, the healings we witness by Jesus's hand spark the belief that leads us to enter into the sacrament with a deeper level of trust.

It is illuminating to compare the grammatical subjects of the ordinary and extraordinary systems as we encounter them in the Gospels. Consider the juxtaposition of the two in Mark 16. Jesus describes the response of faith and reception of the sacraments that follow upon proclamation (the ordinary) with a singular subject: "The *one* who believes and is baptized will be saved" (Mark 16:16; emphasis added). However, when Jesus speaks of the accompanying (extraordinary) signs in the next verse in Mark, the subject changes to plural: "These signs will accompany *those who believe*: in my name *they* will drive out demons, *they* will speak new languages" (Mark 16:17; emphasis added). The transition from singular to plural implies the difference between the individual, concentrated, and pledged action of the ordinary system and the more collective, distributed, and occasional action of the extraordinary system. The effects of the sacraments pertain to *each* believer, and in a certain way, given the disposition of faith, are guaranteed.

In this way, *whoever* believes and is baptized will be saved; we are speaking of an essential promise. On the other hand, signs and wonders accompany the Church as a whole and cannot be forecast. Signs and wonders are not essential to each individual proclamation, but they are integral to the whole of the proclamation. As Newman explains the distinction:

> Whereas final salvation [in Mark 16] is represented as a personal gift, the gift of miracles is not granted here to "*him* that believeth," but to "*them* that believe." And the particular word used, which the Authorized Version translates "follow," suggests or encourages the notion that the miracles promised were to *attend upon* or to be *collateral with* their faith, as general indications and tokens; not indeed that they were to be the result of every act of faith and in every person, but that on the whole, where men were united together by faith in the name of Christ, there miracles would also be wrought by Him who was "in the midst of them."[7]

Miracles and the Goal of Faith

What is the ultimate goal of signs and wonders? To understand miracles as part of the extraordinary system of grace helps us to grasp their *place*, but what is their precise *role*? The positive effects of miracles are manifold: the endorsement of the authority of the missionary, the anticipation of the final times, the display of the invisible through the visible, and the display of the power of God, among others, but we may gather together these various effects and speak of them under a single aspect: the increase of faith! Signs and wonders increase our sense of the presence of God at work among us here and now.

To return to Mark 16: "The Lord Jesus, after he spoke to them, was taken up into heaven and took his seat at the right hand of God. But they went forth and preached everywhere, while the Lord worked with them and confirmed the word through accompanying signs" (Mark 16:19–20). Jesus ascends to sit at the right hand of the Father, the place from which he shares in the glory and honor of the Father. He ascends to intercede for them: as they go out, he remains with them. Imagine the disciples' anxiety, their hesitancy, and their doubt as they embarked upon their mission after the ascension—these disciples who had only ever known ministry while Jesus was leading them in the flesh. They were bound to wonder how Jesus could

7. EM, 209–10.

remain with them after he had departed from them bodily. As they journeyed forth in uncertainty, through the signs they experienced the confirmation of their mission. They were renewed in their confidence. Mark says that the Lord *worked with them*! Peter might have experienced this support as he witnessed miracles through his hands: Jesus, risen from the dead, was with him, giving him a new power to speak and to act.

This pattern of instilling faith or confirmation amidst wavering had already been established during Jesus's earthly ministry. It is the same Lord, possessed of the same power, whether walking among men and women or ascended. Consider the miracle at Cana. After witnessing the water turned into wine, "his disciples began to believe in him" (John 2:11). When Jesus walks towards his disciples on the Sea of Galilee, they proclaim him as the Son of God: "Those who were in the boat did him homage, saying, 'Truly, you are the Son of God'" (Matt 14:33). After Jesus calms a storm, the disciples wonder: "What sort of man is this, whom even the winds and the sea obey?" (Matt 8:27), the implication being that only God possesses such power over the earth. By the same token, miracles in the work of the New Evangelization contribute to the increase of the faith of the missionary. No one is exempt from wavering or doubting: Jesus, in his kindness, sends signs and wonders to his chosen instruments to increase their faith. In the Saint John Society, we can testify to signs and wonders that have renewed us in confidence and joy. When we experience God's goodness in a special way, we often send chronicles to our teams abroad to enhance and strengthen the faith of the whole missionary team.

What applies to disciples and missionaries applies to spiritual seekers as well: signs and wonders bolster faith. For many who are still seeking, they not only lead to renewal but also to conversion: miracles are tools of evangelization. Newman speaks of the role of miracles both in his *Apologia*, as he remarks upon his personal development in faith, as well as in two short essays treating the topic of miracles directly. In both works, he emphasizes how miracles support evangelization: "The Apostles wrought them in evidence of their divine mission; and with this object they have been sometimes wrought by Evangelists of countries since. . . . Hence we hear of them in the history of Saint Gregory in Pontus, and Saint Martin in Gaul; and in their case, as in that of the Apostles, they were both numerous and clear."[8] These miracles open the way for people who otherwise begin without experience and without knowledge of God. As Newman

8. APVS, 165.

puts it, miracles do not only "confirm or encourage the faithful," they also "rouse the attention of unbelievers."[9] We find this to hold true in our own evangelization work. Through a physical healing, the powerful conversion of a friend or family member, or by way of a vision, people come to faith. Perhaps these people appeared to be closed, disinterested, or committed to goals antithetical to the kingdom, but through powerful manifestations of divine agency, the most unlikely prospects come to faith. The seeds of grace sprout with heavy watering.

We can affirm that signs and wonders serve the faith of disciples and seekers alike. However, it is important to know that they do not, as it were, produce something out of nothing; in Newman's terms, they are no remedy for unbelief. Miracles require the soil of faith in order to flourish; they will not yield a harvest if planted on cement. In Nazareth, before a people who rejected his power, Jesus does not perform miracles save for very few (Mark 6:5). At the end of the book of signs in John's Gospel, we hear that people do not come to faith even after having witnessed miracles: "Although he had performed so many signs in their presence, they did not believe in him" (John 12:37). In a manner analogous to his counsel to not throw pearls to swine (Matt 7:6), Jesus denies the scribes and the Pharisees the sign that they request: he says that the only sign he will offer "this faithless generation" is the sign of Jonah, that of his resurrection (Matt 12:38–40). Without openness on the part of his hearers, without the seeds of faith to water, Jesus refuses to work miracles. For us too, miracles are no panacea. Yes, signs and wonders stimulate, renew, and reinforce the process of evangelization. They increase our faith in the resurrected presence of Jesus: this is their very goal. Through signs and wonders, we experience that the Lord is working with us. But they are not all-powerful. Without openness of heart, they make little difference.

Types of Miracles to Expect in the New Evangelization

Which signs and wonders should we expect today? Just as a rising tide lifts all boats, when grace is at work in a community, the anointing of the Spirit takes place, and many manifestations of New Life follow. The growth of the kingdom of God is invariably a multidimensional and holistic reality; there is no such thing as an isolated action of God! In an SSJ working document,

9. APVS, 64.

we list key sites of the manifestation of "the visible signs of the strength of the living and resurrected Christ," including:

- The conversion of the sinner and the change in his or her life (cf. John 4:5–42; 8:1–11).

- The holiness of the just and their progressive configuration with Christ (cf. John 1:35–51; 3:1–13; 21:15–25).

- The presence of signs of the action of God in human life (cf. John 2:1–11; 5:1–9; 6:1–15; 9:1–11; 11:41–44; 20:19–31).

Touched by grace, people reorient their lives, come to resemble Christ, and demonstrate evidence of God's action. To bring these phenomena together, we can list five primary outcomes to expect when we evangelize with power: conversion and spiritual growth, providential events, healings, deliverance, and visions.

First, the conversion of sinners and spiritual growth of the just, though not strictly speaking miracles, are nevertheless manifestations of the supernatural, sure signs of the presence of God. When a notable person in any society, a "big fish" according to whatever reckoning, changes their life, their transformation serves as a reminder far and wide. In Alessandro Manzoni's novel *The Betrothed*, we see an image of the impact of a spectacular conversion on the lives of ordinary people. In the novel, a criminal baron, a sort of proto-mafia boss known only as the Unnamed, had long been inflicting misery on those who lived in his region; his capricious executions and merciless land grabs kept peasants in his territory in a constant state of fear. His hilltop palace, looming like a watchtower above the countryside and surrounded by armed guards, was like a symbol of the unfreedom of the land. The Unnamed's sudden conversion surprised everyone. When he came to repentance with the help of Cardinal Frederigo Borromeo, the news quickly spread. People first shuddered at the thought of him, then whispered that his heart had perhaps truly changed, and at last rejoiced in confidence that Christ had broken through to the most hardened of men. The Unnamed ordered his guards to put away their weapons if they wished to remain in his service; peace came to the region as the Unnamed turned from villain to philanthropist. This example is especially dramatic, but it epitomizes the far-reaching peace that turning to God brings. Among our saints, the turnarounds of Saint Paul and Saint Augustine serve as indelible examples of what God can accomplish in a human being.

It is not only the initial conversion but the entire arc of growth in the spiritual life—the work's beginning and its progress towards completion—that shows forth this power. In our communities, we observe people begin to commit to their neighbors in a new way; we see the luminosity of their witness become more apparent, like the screwing-in of a higher voltage light bulb; and we see people more eager to go out, overcoming personal resistance, to publicly proclaim Christ. This process of transfiguration is an indication of God's presence and action!

Second, we have providential events, which though not technically miracles, are events that reveal the hand of God. When people speak of "God-incidences" as a higher form of coincidences, they are testifying to events that do not exactly fall outside of the range of potential natural explanation, yet are so striking in their timeliness and responsiveness to a particular need that they suggest God's mediation. The moments are varied: it could be a new opportunity that arises in evangelization, the answer to a prayer through an unexpected means, or an encounter with someone—or even the discovery of a book—that renews a person's spiritual life. These are quiet miracles of sorts: regular occurrences from one vantage point, but to the person who sees their inner meaning and uncanny depth, events that reveal God's care.

Newman assesses providential events as those in which God acts not beyond nature but through nature. Without altering or bending the laws of nature, he acts—as if behind the scenes—to steer our course towards his light, to increase our faith and our sense of his presence. Newman writes:

> Grant that upon prayer benefits are vouchsafed, deliverances are effected, unhoped-for success obtained, sickness cured, tempests laid, pestilences put to flight, famines remedied, judgments inflicted, and there will be no need of inquiring into the causes, whether supernatural or natural, to which they are to be referred. They may or they may not, in this or that case, follow or surpass the laws of nature, and they may surpass them plainly or doubtfully, but the common sense of mankind will call them miraculous; for by a miracle, whatever be its formal definition, is popularly meant an event which impresses upon the mind the immediate presence of the Moral Governor of the world. He may sometimes act through nature, sometimes beyond or against it.[10]

10. EM, 252.

In the Saint John Society, we experienced this brand of providential event when we sought to purchase a home near Portland State University as the center for our campus ministry. We had discovered a particular property, evaluated it, and deemed it to be right for our needs, but we found ourselves $50,000 short of the home's price. We had at last lined up a local businessperson from whom to borrow these funds, but as we got closer to the purchase, we began to doubt: was it a good idea to borrow such a large sum for the home? Was our judgment correct after all: was the house perhaps a little too far from the church we were also operating? In short, would this purchase turn out to be a ministerial and financial blunder? But on the day before we had to finalize the deal, we received a call from a longtime friend. He told us that his company had just been sold, and that his boss, a fellow Catholic, wished to donate $50,000 to the Saint John Society! Our prospective purchase was entirely unknown to him. The funds, of course, were immensely helpful in their own right, but they also increased our trust in executing the purchase, precisely at the point at which we were beginning to waver. We don't need to label this event a miracle to detect God's hand in it.

The last three fruits of evangelization with power go together: healings, deliverances, and visions. Newman observes that in the New Testament, these are the most common signs and wonders. Newman sees healings and deliverances as the core signs and wonders of Jesus's promise. He refers to the five signs of Mark 16: driving out demons, speaking in new languages, picking up serpents, drinking poison without being harmed, and healing the sick through the laying-on of hands. He compares these to the four signs Jesus specifies at the beginning of the disciples' ministry in Matt 10. Healing and deliverance are the common elements between the lists:

> First, let it be observed, five gifts are here mentioned as speci-
> mens of our Lord's bequest to His disciples on His departure:
> exorcism, speaking with new tongues, handling serpents, drink-
> ing poison without harm, and healing the sick. When our Lord
> first sent out the Apostles to preach during His ministry, He had
> specified four: "Heal the sick, cleanse the lepers, raise the dead,
> cast out devils." Comparing these two passages together, we find
> that two gifts are common to both of them, and thereby stand
> out as the most characteristic and prominent constituents of the
> supernatural endowment. It is observable, again, that these two
> gifts, of which there is this repeated mention, are not so wonder-
> ful or so decisively miraculous as those of which mention only

occurs in one of the two texts. The power of exorcism and of healing is committed by our Lord to the Apostles, both when He first calls them, and when He is leaving them; but they are promised the gift of tongues only on their second mission, and that of raising the dead only on the first. This does not prove that they could not raise the dead when our Lord had left them; indeed, we know in matter of fact that they had, and that they exercised, the power; but it is natural to suppose that a stress is laid on what is mentioned twice, and to form thence some idea, in consequence, of the predominant character of their miraculous endowment, when it was actually brought into exercise.[11]

Once again, our mission work corroborates Newman's scriptural analysis. We have witnessed countless healings, including the healing from Crohn's disease of one our priests. The healing took place when he was in college: he was discerning for our community, but we recognized that if his debilitating symptoms persisted, he would be unable to take on the grueling work of mission, including stints in rural areas of Argentina with limited medical resources. We decided to pray together for his healing, and God responded: he successfully completed his years of missionary service in Argentina, as well as his priestly education in Washington, DC, and he presently serves with us at a parish in Oregon.

As much physical healing as we have seen, inner healing has been an even more consistent outcome. People testify to us of their healings from resentment, insecurity, lack of meaning, and many other "diseases of the heart." We can bear witness to the freedom people gain as they grow in faith. They break free of the chains of their addictions, obsessions, and co-dependent relationships. When they tell us of their progress, they do not merely infer the work that Christ has done in them: they connect their most significant breakthroughs to retreats, to experiences of prayer, and to the Eucharist. When the kingdom of God grows and the light shines, the forces of darkness have to retreat!

Newman adds a third type of sign to healings and exorcisms: visions. He points out that the Acts of the Apostles is filled not just with healings and deliverances but also visions. He suggests that visions and divine intimations are the characteristic gift of the Acts of the Apostles, the spiritual gift that stimulates and directs the book's action:

11. EM, 82.

St. Peter opens the sacred history of the Acts with a reference to the Prophet Joel's promise of the time, when "their sons and their daughters should prophesy, and their young men should see visions, and their old men should dream dreams"; an announcement of which the narrative which follows abundantly records the fulfilment. St. Stephen sees our Lord before his martyrdom; the Angel directs St. Philip to go towards Gaza, and the Holy Spirit Himself bids him join himself to the Ethiopian's chariot; St. Paul is converted by a vision of our Lord; St. Peter has the vision of the clean and unclean beasts, and Cornelius is addressed by an Angel; Angels release first the Apostles, then St. Peter from prison; "a vision appeared to Paul in the night, there stood a man of Macedonia"; at Corinth Christ "spoke to Paul in the night by a vision, Be not afraid"; Agabus and St. Philip's four daughters prophesy; in prison "the Lord stood by Paul, and said, Be of good cheer"; on board ship an Angel stood by him, saying, "Fear not, Paul, thou must be brought before Caesar" (Acts vii. 56; viii. 26, 29; ix. 3–6; x. 3, 10, etc.).[12]

Visions have surfaced in especially dramatic ways in our ministerial experience. A woman in her forties from our San Juan Diego community in Oregon went through a harrowing trial after contracting COVID-19. Once she fell sick, her condition deteriorated rapidly, and she went into a coma. The doctors were nearly certain that she would not survive. Fellow members of the San Juan Diego community organized to pray outside the hospital, planting themselves directly beneath her room on the fourth floor. Their hours-long vigil moved several nurses and doctors to tears. This woman was in a coma for nearly two months, but she showed strong enough vital signs that the doctors continued working to keep her alive. Amazingly, she emerged from the coma: she is now back to functioning normally, and she is profoundly grateful to be alive.

She says she does not remember the period during her coma, except for a vision she experienced. She saw herself alone in a desert, strapped to a chair. She cried out to God, yelling, "God, why me? There are terrible criminals out there, there are thieves, there are serial abusers, there are even murderers. . . . Why am *I* going through this? Why are you holding me captive?" At that moment, Jesus approached her from across the desert sands, and said, "There may be murderers out there, but you kill with your tongue!" At that, she came face to face with her guilt and

---

12. EM, 84.

repented. The figure of Jesus released her from the straps wound around her. Upon waking up, she set it upon herself to begin to make amends for the wounds she had caused through her harsh words. From her hospital room, she called those she believed she had offended and asked for forgiveness. Many of the people she called were so moved that they too began to apologize to her. She shared that she feels as if she spends her days now at the juncture of heaven and earth. She has tasted the goodness of God through her healing—and just as much through the reconciliation in her life that God inspired through it.

We all should report stories like those recounted in this chapter: stories of God's remarkable providence, of healings, and of visions. Our testimony brings glory to God. As Newman points out, healings, exorcisms, and visions actually fall within the category of less spectacular supernatural mighty deeds, when compared with raising the dead, nature miracles (like walking on water), and drinking poison without ill effect. Yet who would question that these kinds of signs and wonders inspire awe? They are especially useful for the work of mission, as they are conjoined with the proclamation of the gospel and integral to the spiritual growth of the Christian.

Application: Signs and Wonders in your Personal Mission

1. Be open to the supernatural action of God! As our society on the whole becomes progressively more closed to the notion of supernatural action, God seeks to lift up beneficiaries and witnesses to his power. Consider the testimony of Marian apparitions, healings, and the eucharistic miracles. Pray that you may encounter the Lord acting with power today.

2. When you are gifted, bear witness. In the Old Testament, after God heals Tobit of his blindness, the archangel Raphael appears to him, exhorting him to testify to the action of God: "Proclaim before all with due honor the deeds of God, and do not be slack in thanking him. A king's secret should be kept secret, but one must declare the works of God and give thanks with due honor" (Tob 12:6–7). Testify to the deeds of God. Be prompt in thanking him! As Newman writes, "What He does in secret, we must think over in secret; what He has 'openly

showed in the sight of the heathen,' we must publish abroad, 'crying aloud, and sparing not.'"[13]

3. Pray for miracles: ask for the intercession of saints. Saints are acquainted with miracles, both through their earthly life and in their intercessory position in heaven.

4. Translate your awe to the "ordinary" system, the system of the sacraments. God's care for us in the day-to-day is no less marvelous than his outsized works of glory. Ponder the meaning of the eucharistic gift and of the gift of the sacrament of penance, where God unfailingly shows up and bestows his mercy.

13. EM, 230.

CHAPTER EIGHT

Personal Influence: The Interpersonal Element in the Act of Faith

Introduction: The Rain, the Stone, and How the Water Flows

SINCERE MISSIONARIES, BUOYED BY the experience of seeing hearts turn to Christ, invariably come to ask: How can we reach more people? How can we draw more to conversion? We may be tempted to think that there remains a certain strategy, an untried approach, by which we can reach the masses quickly and effectively. Neither the example set by Jesus nor the historical record of evangelization indicates the feasibility of a single catchall tactic. Only the humble and dedicated commitment of fervent disciples has proven to lie at the heart of the spread of Christianity: above all, Christianity has grown—at turns rapid and gradual, both dramatically advancing and steadily, quietly unfolding—through the personal influence of those who believe.

For Saint John Henry Newman, this idea emerged as a kind of personal theological passion. In his university sermon, delivered at Oxford, "Personal Influence, the Means of Propagating the Truth," he directly asks the question about the transmission of Catholic faith across time: How did the Catholic truth prevail throughout history? In addition to the assistance of the Holy Spirit, can we find any rational explanation for the propagation of Christianity? Newman discards the explanations of political power, the presence of miracles, and the progressive flowering of ideas as inadequate. He proposes that the only sufficient explanation is the heart-to-heart transmission of the faith: "I answer, that [Christianity] has been upheld in the world not as a system, not by books, not by argument, nor by temporal power, but by the personal influence of such men . . . who are at once the teachers and the patterns of it."[1]

This notion of personal influence is a central, irreplaceable element of the work of evangelization. We could alternatively name this *p* the *p* of Presence. Presence cannot be replicated by any other means. Just as a father cannot hand off the concrete, incarnate task of parenting without hurting his child, an evangelizer cannot rely on an instrumentalization of evangelization without shortchanging his or her audience. Where communities of faith flourish, we find commitment to *presence*, to knowing others and being known, to love as the practice of everyday life.

To define our key term more precisely: we understand personal influence to mean the impact that a person exercises upon another person through direct contact. In Spanish, the word is *influir*: to flow into. Leadership, viewed holistically, can be understood as the flow of the vision of the leader into the wider body, person by person. We need not look for the moment or exchange when the influence occurs: the largely unconscious transmission of ideas, principles, and values takes place through regular interaction. Through conversation, time spent together, and implicit communication of lifestyle, a person gradually comes to make their mark on another. The transmission of faith happens the same way: faith is transmitted, in a phrase most precious to Newman, by way of *heart speaking to heart*. A believer firmly rooted in his or her faith begins to exercise a silent influence upon all those who are around him. His worldview, ideas, sensibility, and above all *love* start to permeate and flow into the lives of those who share life with him or her.

We put forth this approach as the most full-bodied form of evangelization, the method that imitates Christ most exactly and comprehensively. For each missionary, personal influence is essential, but another method involving presence remains pivotal in its own right: public evangelization has its place, as it did for Jesus, who addressed crowds in addition to his disciples. If we were to picture these two methods of transmission, we could identify public evangelization as *the way of the falling of the rain* and personal influence as *the way of the tossing of the stone*. We must develop systems for evangelization (to bring down the rain): occasional events and public lectures, faith formation programs of every stripe, social media ministries for the unaffiliated, etc. The essential condition of a ministry of presence does not deny the need for discipleship of range.

1. PI, para. 26.

Yet, the rain has its limits. Public evangelization is invariably limited by its indiscriminateness, the method of addressing the crowds rather than the individual. We must find a way to keep the faces in the crowd from remaining unrecognized; we must drive forward from breadth into depth; intimacy must come to supplant extension. This is where personal influence takes over, even on the heels to publicly evangelize. The way of personal influence may be slow. The number of people we reach through personal proximity may be very few. But it has the outstanding merit of reaching people with intensity and calibration. And this intensity bears within itself an expansive nature.

Personal influence introduces a powerful flow of energy into the world. Influence passes effectively beyond the first person, reaching some people nearby with more immediacy and others more indirectly, like the stone tossed into a lake, possessed of a center of impact, making a splash in one place but causing ripples that radiate outward. Yet, when each person is reached—no matter how far from the center—he or she experiences a relationship that bespeaks the depth of communion with Christ. Not only does personal influence begin with a one-on-one encounter and grow to encompass a wider field of relations, but this field becomes bound securely by genuine personal relationship. This is one reason why the ostensibly slow and small-scale method is precisely the method by which the name of Christ has canvassed the world.

The Method of the Master: Incarnational Evangelization

Whatever its foundations in practical wisdom, the concept of personal influence finds its ultimate ground beyond day-to-day relationships in the way that God has shared himself with human beings. Simply put, personal influence describes the way God relates with us—by emptying himself totally and bridging the infinite gap in order for him to encounter us *as one of us*. The incarnation of Jesus Christ becomes the archetype and the source for the interpersonal encounters that mediate faith.

The notion of personal relationship is familiar also in the Old Testament, wherein God's relationship with Israel is variously characterized as a husband's love for his wife (the book of Hosea), a mother's love for her child (Isa 49:15), and a parent's undying love for the child whom the parent once taught to walk, took up into their arms, and bent down to feed (Hos 11:3–4). With these analogies, the Bible frames God's relationship to Israel—and, as the story unfolds, to all of humanity—in interpersonal language: tenderness, care, and fidelity are integral to God's way of seeing and relating to human beings. In the New Testament, we no longer depend upon metaphorical statements about God's personal relationship to humanity: rather, God relates to us directly, not *conceived of as a person* (in the mode of a father, mother, or husband), nor *in the way a person would* (paternally, maternally, etc.), but *as* the person of Jesus.

Like rain that falls on everyone, Jesus's message came down upon crowds. But he addressed these crowds while traveling with his small band of disciples whom he was constantly forming. Through their time together, taken up in public ministry, personal fellowship, and prayer, Jesus communicated his mind and heart to his disciples.

Newman considers Jesus's committed term of formation of his disciples as a logical necessity: no other method would have been effective to spread the gospel. He argues as follows: in order for Jesus to be certain of the transmission of the gospel, he required loyal, enduring witnesses to his resurrection. Otherwise, no matter the glory of the event, the frailty of human nature would reassert itself: chance witnesses would move on to other things, and the saving message would die out. In order to assure constancy in witness, he needed to school a select band; he needed to call together a group and instruct them for an intensive period. For his purpose, mere contact would not do, and even intimate affection would not be enough—nothing short of the steady impress of his being upon theirs would suffice. Newman writes:

> [They were not] required merely to know Him, but the thought of Him was to be stamped upon their minds as the one master-spring of their whole course of life for the future. But men are not easily wrought upon to be faithful advocates of any cause. Not only is the multitude fickle: but the best men, unless urged, tutored, disciplined to their work, give way; untrained nature has no principles.[2]

Jesus's method was to choose a small group of disciples and through them reach others. We can call this the "ripple effect" of evangelization. The stone lands in the pond in one place, and the waves begin to flow out. This effect is notable in the public life of Jesus and above all in the time of Pentecost.

In chapter 1 of John's Gospel, Andrew, after meeting Jesus, goes out to find his brother Simon Peter, telling him that he has found the Messiah (John

2. WR, 1:183–84.

1:41). Next, Philip shares the same discovery with the skeptical Nathanael, who then comes to Jesus to verify for himself (John 1:46–51). In chapter 4 of John's Gospel, the Samaritan woman whom Jesus meets by the well invites her whole town to approach Jesus. During his public life, Jesus nurtures the disciples in order to pass the torch of faith along.

This dynamism of Jesus's personal influence attains its fulfillment on Pentecost day. John writes that Jesus breathed his Spirit upon the disciples (John 20:22). Breath is the symbol of the life force of an individual; it is by way of the breath that any word can even be shared. All that Jesus is, all that he thinks, how he loves—all of this, he communicates to the disciples through his breathing forth of the Holy Spirit, *his* Spirit. The influence is so powerful that the disciples are able to imitate his deeds and way of life—to become like him. They receive the Spirit, and they begin to proclaim like him. The ripple effect continues without end, to the present day.

In a Church that understands the transmission of faith as an unbroken line flowing forth from Jesus onto his disciples, and then far and wide, this storyline is much more than a historical artifact that mirrors our own person-to-person sharing of faith. This history of faith also represents the very taproot of our own endeavor, revealing to us the line of persons to whom we are indebted. The method of the master becomes our own today only because others have carried to us the message that, at the dawn of the first millennium, first fell from the master's lips.

The Method of the Master in the Life of the Saint: Personal Influence Embodied through Newman

In the Catholic tradition, John Henry Newman is the great articulator of the concept of personal influence. He learned about Jesus's method as much by his own experience as by explicit study of the New Testament. He formed his understanding throughout his life, drawing from observation of the essential factors in his own development and the development of the faithful Christians he knew. In his autobiography, *Apologia pro Vita Sua*, he traces the reciprocal influence of close companions on his thinking. He notes that while living in regular contact with friends and pupils in the university atmosphere at Oxford, he always found himself in relationships of mutual development. Newman writes, "At no time have I acted upon others, without their acting upon me."[3] These close relationships became

3. APVS, 75.

the means of dissemination of his own theological ideas; not according to an explicit program or by sustained instruction, but rather by the force of enthusiasm, his ideas took root:

> It was through friends, younger, for the most part, than myself, that my principles were spreading. They heard what I said in conversation and told it to others. Undergraduates in due time took their degree, and became private tutors themselves. In this new status, in turn, they preached the opinions which they had already learned themselves. Others went down to the country, and became the curate of parishes. Then they had down from London parcels of the Tracts and other publications. They placed them in the shops of local booksellers, got them into newspapers, introduced them to clerical meetings.[4]

In each of the phases of his life, Newman exemplified the priority of the person-to-person passage of ideas, virtues, and faith. As a tutor at Oxford from 1826 to 1832, he chafed against the expectations that tutors remain aloof from their students and act as remote purveyors and elucidators of academic material. He felt that the deeper call of the role was to accompany the totality of the person—to commit to each student as an individual and to enter into the student's concerns and strivings. Starting with this foundational relationship, he reasoned, he could then offer deeper formation in line with a spiritual vision of his task. In a letter to a friend, he expressed his frustrations about the clamp exercised on his efforts to fulfill this vision: "There is much in the system which I think wrong; I think the tutors see too little of the men, and there is not enough of direct religious instruction. It is my wish to consider myself a minister of Christ. I find that opportunities occur of doing spiritual good to those over whom I am placed, it will become a grave question whether I ought to continue in the Tuition."[5] Newman's disagreements led him to renounce the position. Though he moved on, Newman did not forget his early standpoint: when assigned to develop a Catholic university in Ireland, he retained his conviction that tutors should live alongside students. Newman conceived of these tutors as agents of academic instruction, of personal renewal, and of spiritually beneficial influence.

Though Newman gave up his position as tutor, he remained at Oxford until 1841, where he stood at the center of the Oxford Movement, formed

---

4. APVS, 75.

5. Newman, journal entry, 1826. Further bibliographic information unavailable.

by a group of Anglican clerics eager to reform and revitalize the decadent Anglican Church. He authored tracts—small essays aimed towards vigorous defense and transmission of the movement's principles. In his *Apologia*, reflecting on the Oxford Movement, he again considered the conditions necessary for intellectual development, accounting networks of relationships among the like-minded as the hidden key to advance: "Living movements do not come of committees, nor are great ideas worked out through the post.... Universities are the natural centers of intellectual movements. How could men act together, whatever was their zeal, unless they were united in a sort of individuality?"[6] Newman emphasized that the condition for success of intellectual movements was a shared life, not only by way of location but, more crucially, through a unity borne of "a common history, common memories, an intercourse of mind with mind in the past, and a progress and intercourse of that intercourse in the present."[7]

After this intensive period at Oxford, fueled by the close network of collaborative relationships and study of the church fathers, Newman became unable to reconcile his evolving theological commitments with his adherence to Anglicanism. He sensed that no reform would be able to redirect the Church according to the vision that had grown in him of the fullness of Christian truth, and he withdrew to the neighboring district of Littlemore to embark upon a course of deepened prayer and meditation. He leased a former mail coach staging post, transforming a long building of offices into a spare house, the post's stable into a library, and the barn into cottages to lodge his friends. He and his friends took up a semimonastic life of prayer, study, and fasting. This quiet four-year period (1841–45) at Littlemore nurtured his conversion. It was here, surrounded by a company of his close friends, that Newman broke through his lingering resistances and was received into the Catholic Church. Littlemore represents not only the culmination of his conversion but, moreover, the point of maturation of his model of education and spiritual formation: in this tight band of friends dedicated to holiness, pursuing the truth, cultivating virtue, and seeking God in prayer, Newman found within himself a peace and confidence that enabled him to journey out from his familiar intellectual and spiritual world and into the Church.

Two years after entering the Church, Newman became a priest and joined the Oratory of Saint Philip Neri. In Saint Philip, Newman found the

6. APVS, 59–60.

7. APVS, 59–60.

very embodiment of his long-gestating ideas about personal influence. He wrote, "St. Philip, like St. Paul, wanted to influence by personal sympathy and love rather than by command."[8] Saint Philip's method thus spoke to his own teaching and experience at Oxford and Littlemore, marking the flowering of the conviction that nothing substitutes for "the intercourse of soul with soul, the play of mind upon mind."[9]

When Pope Leo XIII named him a cardinal in 1879, Newman chose as his motto the famous phrase of Saint Francis de Sales: *Cor ad cor loquitur*, translated as "heart speaks to heart." Originally, the phrase pertains to the relationship between the Sacred Heart of Jesus and the human heart—the heart of the Lord speaking to the depths, calling to holiness, and guiding to the Father. However, "heart speaks to heart" can also describe a kind of pastoral charity wherein a person leads another to God through love and kindness, expressing Newman's belief that next to the power of supernatural grace, the greatest influence over the human soul is the example of goodness in another person. The motto epitomizes his lifelong spiritual journey, and the conclusion he had been tending towards at every stage, whether at Oxford, Littlemore, or as a Catholic priest in the many locations he ministered—the conclusion that the heart of Christ, charged with love for all humankind, finds its foremost earthly expression through the friendship of men and women dedicated to him, and through him, to one another.

Principles within Personal Influence

The Holiness Principle: The Saint as the Interpreter of the Word of God

Newman insists that the truth is propagated most powerfully through the example of teachers who embody what they teach—those exemplary teachers who are also witnesses, to use Pope Paul VI's expression from *Evangelii Nuntiandi*. In the portrait Newman draws of this type, he points to the essential difference between the spiritually alive person on one hand (epitomized by the saint) and those models of human excellence with which we are more familiar:

---

8. Quoted in Van Den Bergh, "Cardinal Newman."
9. Quoted in Van Den Bergh, "Cardinal Newman."

We shall find it difficult to estimate the moral power which a single individual, trained to practice what he teaches, may acquire in his own circle, in the course of years. While the Scriptures are thrown upon the world, as if the common property of any who choose to appropriate them, he is, in fact, the legitimate interpreter of them, and none other; the Inspired Word being but a dead letter (ordinarily considered), except as transmitted from one mind to another. While he is unknown to the world, yet, within the range of those who see him, he will become the object of feelings different in kind from those which mere intellectual excellence excites. The men commonly held in popular estimation are greatest at a distance; they become small as they are approached; but the attraction, exerted by unconscious holiness, is of an urgent and irresistible nature; it persuades the weak, the timid, the wavering, and the inquiring; it draws forth the affection and loyalty of all who are in a measure like-minded; and over the thoughtless or perverse multitude it exercises a sovereign compulsory sway, bidding them fear and keep silence, on the ground of its own right divine to rule them,—its hereditary claim on their obedience, though they understand not the principles or counsels of that spirit, which is "born, not of blood, nor of the will of the flesh, nor of the will of man, but of God."[10]

Newman affirms the power of the saint, the inimitable holy person who has transformative power over his or her circle. For Newman, *the saint is the interpreter of the word of God.* The saint's special capacity to interpret the Scriptures, to hear God's word free from impediment, lies in their configuration to Christ. All else—even scholarly erudition—can rightly be considered of secondary value. The saint is distinguished by an unmistakable relationship to God that is elevated above all that is worldly, all that can be known, imagined, or reverse engineered according to a natural and comprehensible process. The three transcendentals become unified in the light of the saint's presence—a quality that must be experienced to be understood. We might say that the difference between sanctity and any other form of excellence is that even if some other excellence is difficult to attain, people can generally place it—they can explain it—whereas the saint radiates an attractive and irresistible mystery. The vital message comes through: *the saint validates the reality of the kingdom of God.*

The impact of unconscious holiness helps us to understand the importance of raising up sincere disciples in our Church today. Only when

10. PI, para. 33.

people see the holiness of a person or of a community—only when they encounter real and concrete witness—can they grasp the truth of Christianity. Once people perceive this light, they seek to assimilate it for themselves. As former Communion and Liberation president Julian Carron likes to say, tongue in cheek, "The power of Christianity lies in envy." Holiness is persuasive. It is contagious. It changes the direction of lives, while it confirms those already on the course. These interpersonal factors become an added source of motivation behind drawing close to Jesus—not only the intimacy that one gains for oneself. As Newman demonstrates in his meditation "Jesus, Light of the Soul," we achieve the consummation of our spiritual lives through selflessly transmitting the gifts we have first been given:

> Stay with me, and then I shall begin to shine as Thou shinest: so to shine as to be a light to others. The light, O Jesus, will be all from Thee. None of it will be mine. No merit to me. It will be Thou who shinest through me upon others. O let me thus praise Thee, in the way which Thou dost love best, by shining on all those around me. Give light to them as well as to me; light them with me, through me.[11]

The Sphere of Influence Principle: Holiness Recognized

The holiness that shines from one life to another can only be perceived with a certain proximity. Only when you are close to someone can you see their inner self and their deepest orientation towards life. As Newman points out, intimate relationships offer the sole clear window through which the integrity of a person becomes visible. The holy person can be known only by coming close; otherwise, we cannot cut through the mirage of the public persona. Newman writes:

> Of course in proportion as persons are brought out into public life, they will be seen and scrutinized, and (in a certain sense) known more; but I am talking of the ordinary condition of people in private life, such as our Savior was for thirty years; and these look very like each other. And there are so many of them, that unless we get very near them, we cannot see any distinction between one and another; we have no means to do so, and it is no business of ours. And yet, though we have no right to judge others, but must leave this to God, it is very certain that a really holy man, a

11. MD, 363.

true saint, though he looks like other men, still has a sort of secret power in him to attract others to him who are like-minded, and to influence all who have anything in them like him.[12]

When we ponder the curiosity people often display regarding the private lives of celebrities, we become witness to a kind of naïve, inchoate, but nevertheless telling desire to behold a whole-souled human being. People naturally wonder whether the inner reflects the outer, and the more impressive the outer person, the more they seek to discover whether their unspoken image of a more complete and more fulfilled being is merely an image, a fantasy, or reflects some attainable human state. People wonder whether the admired celebrity treats their family well, carries on loving relationships, and possesses personal integrity. At the most basic level, though they would likely not be conscious of the question, they might just be asking: *Is this person whom I admire holy?* Is there something more, something that suggests a greater power and depth, behind the public-facing mask of the "impressive" human being? Now, especially with celebrities, we are accustomed to presuming a great discrepancy between image and reality, and we are pleasantly surprised if we detect any correspondence between the two. What an amazing gift when, in the course of life, we meet someone who grows in stature the more that we know them, who demonstrates more love and concern in private than before an audience, and who holds sincerely to the articles of faith that they profess before others. Usually, this is the situation that we do not expect—and the discovery that fills us with appreciation: it is an encounter with saintliness.

The Leadership Principle: From the Few to the Many

A third element of the principle of personal influence is the leadership principle. God reaches the many through the few. As we remarked before, we see this exemplified both in the Old Testament, wherein God chooses Israel to reach out to all nations, and in the method of the master in the New Testament, wherein Jesus trains a small band of disciples to reach all nations. This is how God works, a "general characteristic of his providence," as Newman calls it.[13] The few serve as channels of blessing for the many.

12. PPS, 244.
13. WR, 1:183.

But additionally, as we touched upon earlier, Jesus's method is determined by the earthly realities of his ministry and resurrection. In order to bear witness to his resurrection, his disciples needed to know him—but not only know him, also to be certain it was he who was risen, and moreover be so impacted by him as to make his life, death, and resurrection the focus of their lives thereafter. There could be only so many people to fit this bill! Recollect Newman's sermon "Witnesses to the Resurrection," when he asks why, after Jesus's resurrection, he appeared not to the crowds but only to a small group. He argues from this principle of the few to the many: "It would seem, then, that our Lord gave His attention to a few, because, if the few be gained, the many will follow. To these few He showed Himself again and again. These He restored, comforted, warned, inspired. He formed them unto Himself, that they might show forth His praise."[14]

The personal influence approach comes most into its own when connected explicitly with the formation of disciples. This formation exists both for the sake of the disciple being formed and for the sake of all whom this person will one day reach. Just as Jesus invested in a small group and through this group reached those he could not meet immediately, our ministries flourish by the force of multiplication. We must bear in mind that our field of influence is not restricted to our field of vision! In our time also, the Lord reaches the many through the few. Today, the effective pattern to follow is to train disciples and then train these disciples to be disciple-makers. We are gifted in order to gift others, and we do not diminish but rather grow in the act.

Living Out Personal Influence

The principle of personal influence indicates the primacy of a grounded faith life. Lived relationship must come first—prior to what we might fairly label as our collective addiction to digesting current events and forming opinions. The slogan "form relationships before opinions" may be a healthy corrective for the Church today. Through humble connection, we can do our part to overcome the rancor that grows wherever judgments become more strident and factions entrenched. Through humble connection, we effectively dial down the heat in the sweltering room of public exchange. Not only do we become agents of healing, but we experience healing ourselves. Through embracing relationship—and particularly

14. WR, 1:184..

through establishing breadth of connection—we are healed of the severity, of the habitual incredulousness, of the indignation and offense that tend to sneak up and take root within our present society.

The first step to integrate the wisdom of personal influence is simple: eagerness to relate and trust in the good of relationship. Here are five more practical corollaries to help you assimilate this principle.

Invest in Your Spiritual Life: The Impact of the Testimony of Life

Both the Scriptures and pastoral experience show forth the importance of testimony of life. Presence and proclamation are closely connected: the power of testimony confirms and renders tangible the word announced. In the Saint John Society, we like to say that people *live, irradiate,* and *announce* the new situation in Christ. To live means to live a consistent or integrated Christian life; to irradiate means to inspire through the force of attraction of conformity to Christ; and to announce means to explicitly proclaim the gospel and what Christ has done for you. Testimony includes not only the verbal report of Christ, but rather the whole integral picture of life that a Christian communicates, as *Evangelii Nuntiandi* expresses:

> Above all the Gospel must be proclaimed by witness. Take a Christian or a handful of Christians who, in the midst of their own community, show their capacity for understanding and acceptance, their sharing of life and destiny with other people, their solidarity with the efforts of all for whatever is noble and good. Let us suppose that, in addition, they radiate in an altogether simple and unaffected way their faith in values that go beyond current values, and their hope in something that is not seen and that one would not dare to imagine. Through this wordless witness these Christians stir up irresistible questions in the hearts of those who see how they live: Why are they like this? Why do they live in this way? What or who is it that inspires them? Why are they in our midst? Such a witness is already a silent proclamation of the Good News and a very powerful and effective one. Here we have an initial act of evangelization.[15]

Pope Paul's assessment reads like a gloss on Jesus's exhortation in the Sermon on the Mount: "Let your light shine before others, that they may see your good deeds and glorify your heavenly Father" (Matt 5:16). The

---

15. EN, para. 21.

testimony of life speaks to those outside of Christianity; here is the communication of Christianity by way of "envy," as Julian Carron put it. As one of our parishioners remarked, "People come to Christ because he is the Truth, so there's no need to embellish what you're doing in your faith or what your faith has done for you. If you're experiencing great joy in Christ, speak about it. If you're suffering, speak about it and proclaim the hope you have in Christ. People can argue points of theology, but no one can argue against your personal experience."

Our own life of holiness speaks as nothing else can. The person of sanctity remains anchored to the supernatural, driven on daily by the things above and driving others towards the light of the unseen world. As Newman writes, for the saintly person,

> the course of each day is religious: while other children are light-minded, and cannot fix their thoughts in prayer, prayer and praise and meditation are his meat and drink. He frequents the Churches, and places himself before the Blessed Sacrament: or he is found before some holy image; or he sees visions of the Blessed Virgin, or of the Saints to whom he is devoted. He lives in intimate converse with his guardian Angel, and he shrinks from the very shadow of profaneness or impurity. And thus, he is a special witness of the world unseen, and he fulfils the vague ideas and the dreams of the supernatural, which one reads of in poems or romances, with which young people are so much taken, and after which they cannot help sighing, before the world corrupts them. . . . There is but one real Antagonist of the world, and that is the faith of Catholics;—Christ set that faith up, and it will do its work on earth, as it ever has done, till He comes again.[16]

The supernatural anchoring of the Christian spills over into everyday life. A committed disciple from our Portland community expressed how her spiritual life was noticed by her supervisor, not in the form of her public piety but in her service as a nurse:

> Today I had my mid-semester review for my clinical internship. I have been assigned to a chronic care facility where the majority of the population are elder adults with chronic diseases. My task is to help them manage their suffering. My instructor mentioned that I have displayed immense growth and receptivity to the feedback that I have been given throughout the term and that my desire to mature and grow as a nurse is unlike the other students.

16. DMC, "Discourse 5," 96–97, 103.

He mentioned how he has often pondered why I am different, since everyone else professes a desire for growth and to receive feedback. He continued to emphasize this mystery of depth that I display in the clinical setting. As he spoke, I knew exactly what was different: it was Christ. Living as an active disciple changes everything. It has changed the way that I look at the career ahead of me because it changes the way that I see each person that I encounter. It changes the way that I desire growth and improvement because it is not for my own gain but for the glory of God in me. It changes the way I respond to adversity, challenge, and criticism because all is for Christ, with Christ, and like Christ. I am absolutely amazed at the feedback I received, not because I am proud of the work I am doing in clinical, but because it has edified me as a disciple. It was so clear to me that, in that moment, it was no longer me but Christ in me being noticed and praised by my instructor. I was able to drive home from clinical repeating what the instructor said to me but redirecting it to the One who deserves to hear it. The source of all that is good in me is Christ! The work that is being done is Christ, it is only Christ!

Invest in your spiritual life! This will allow you to bear the fruit of a transformed humanity, to be a normal person yet with the fruits of the Holy Spirit present in your life. You will irradiate Christ. Others will take note of the love, peace, joy, and authenticity that has taken root in your life.

Foster the Apostolate of Friendship

We like to say that friends inviting friends is the most effective method of evangelization. Friendship and trust are operative along the whole journey of faith. Remember that "trust in a Christian" is the first of the thresholds of faith. People may have been away from the Church or institutional religion, but the friendship or personal contact with a Christian might provide the spark to trigger a faith journey. Those who are already seeking can also be moved ahead on the path of discipleship by the testimony of a friend who is more committed than they are to faith. We call this the Barnabas principle, alluding to how Barnabas personally brought Paul to the apostles to draw him into the life of the early Church. The same principle applies in sacramental preparation and initiation: in RCIA, candidates select sponsors to support them in their confirmation and catechumens choose godparents for their baptism. When preparing to baptize their children, parents choose godparents. Many churches appoint sponsor couples for marriages as well. The conviction behind these relationships is double: in the first place, God's call, which brings forth companions for the journey of faith, and in the second, the unity of the body of Christ, sustained through the sympathy and support offered to Christ's members.

Holiness engenders holiness! Even committed disciples need encouragement. In his providence, God sends us friends in Christ to help us grow. Historically, we observe that pairs of saints, either friends or relatives, grew together in holiness. Benedict and Scholastica, Francis and Clare, and Teresa of Avila and John of the Cross are all pairs who together changed the trajectory of Catholic spirituality. Close friends Saint Basil the Great and Saint Gregory of Nazianzus (Gregory referred to them as "two bodies with a single spirit"[17]) paved the path for the formulation of the doctrine of the Holy Trinity in the early Church, while Ignatius of Loyola and Francis Xavier together directed and pioneered the transmission of the gospel to the New World. In families, there is the example of Monica, whose son Augustine credits her fervent prayer for his conversion, and Louise and Zelie Martin, parents of Therese of Lisieux and four additional daughters who became nuns. Saint Irenaeus of Lyon traces his personal encouragement back to the source. See here his letter to Victor, testifying to the transmission of faith from heart to heart:

> When I was still a boy, I saw you in Lower Asia in Polycarp's company. . . . I have a clearer recollection of events at that time than of recent happenings—what we learn in childhood develops along with the mind and becomes part of it—so that I can describe the place where blessed Polycarp sat and talked, his goings out and comings in, the character of his life, his personal appearance, his addresses to the crowded congregations. I remember how he spoke of his intercourse with John and with the other who had seen the Lord; how he repeated their words from memory; and how the things he had heard them say about the Lord, his miracles and His teaching, things that he had heard directly from the eye-witnesses of the Word of Life, were proclaimed by Polycarp in complete harmony with Scripture. To these things I listened eagerly at that time, by the mercy of God shown to me, not committing them to writing but learning them by heart. By God's grace, I constantly ruminate on them.[18]

---

17. Gregory Nazianzen, "Oration 43," §20.

18. Irenaeus, "Letter to Florinus," in Eusebius, "Writings of Irenaeus."

Bloom Where You Are Planted: Evangelization in the Square Space

Recall the sphere of influence principle: only through proximity can we discover holiness. The practical corollary is that we must evangelize in our sphere of influence, not dream of going somewhere else. Even in the age of worldwide mission, the Church has consistently emphasized the importance of evangelizing within your sphere of influence. We already have connections with family, neighbors, and co-workers: Why begin anywhere else? Even strangers living in the same city fall within our orbit, whether we see them regularly on the same transit route or bump into them only once. We must not be asleep to the opportunities that arise in the ordinary moments of our days. In *Evangelii Gaudium*, Pope Francis calls explicitly for this humble readiness: "Being a disciple means being constantly ready to bring the love of Jesus to others, and this can happen unexpectedly and in any place: on the street, in a city square, during work, on a journey."[19] Except in rare cases, our inclination need not be towards the missionary expedition; we need not be hankering to set off for distant lands in imitation of Saint Francis Xavier and the early Jesuits. We are useful here at home; we do not have to go far to find our "Indias" in need of evangelization. Plant the tree where you are grounded; reach out to those nearby. Let us not be like the person who says he loves humanity with a pure heart, the only problem being that he cannot stand any of his neighbors!

Once we find ourselves rooted in our sphere of influence, we will be able to influence others, one heart at a time. This will be a slow but powerful source of transformation. As Newman writes:

> He who obeys God conscientiously, and lives holily, forces all about him to believe and tremble before the unseen power of Christ . . . to his neighbors he manifests the Truth in proportion to their knowledge of him; and some of them, through God's blessing, catch the holy flame, cherish it, and in their turn transmit it. And thus in a dark world Truth still makes way in spite of the darkness, passing from hand to hand.[20]

The holy flame is passed on one by one, heart to heart, one soul at a time. The notion of evangelization by proximity might at first seem to imply that evangelization proceeds more slowly than we would hope. It is

19. EG, 127.
20. WR, 1:187.

not like the blog or video that, at least hypothetically, possesses a virtually limitless reach. Neither does personal evangelization have the neatness of a predictable, prepackaged product. Since we are presenting ourselves to another person, we are necessarily showing ourselves in vulnerability and incompleteness: a raw side of us will invariably emerge. But in this limitation lies the integrity, the realism, the very power of the method, most attractive not for its flash but for its authenticity. We must meet our small circles with the confidence that personal holiness and holiness alone will bear fruit, as well as the faith that God does not leave us alone in our efforts. We need not eschew programs that reach crowds through social media, public preaching, and videos. The rain that falls on all has its place. But we should also trust that the splash made by the singular rock—hewn or unhewn—cannot be replicated, and that the subsequent ripples travel farther than the eye can see.

To make the most of the opportunities in your sphere is to rediscover the capacity for renewal, joy, and development in the circumstances of your own life. It is to be faithful to the primacy of the rock over the rain in the life of evangelization, which maintains the integrity of your mission. Be attentive, as God may send people your way and ask you to act. An employee of a construction company who has been through our programs describes one such moment:

> I was sitting at my desk at work the other day and saw my project manager walk into his office. I felt a strong prompting that I should invite him to Alpha. Now, my project manager is also one of the vice presidents of my company, so it was a super intimidating idea that I should talk to him about faith. I said a quick prayer and told God that I was scared to talk to my project manager, but if He really wanted me to, I would go do it. I looked up the Gospel for the day and lo and behold, the Gospel was Mark 16:15–18: "Go into the whole world and proclaim the gospel to every creature. . . . " God was practically screaming at me to go evangelize. I looked up from my desk and saw that my project manager was alone in his office and figured that this was my opportunity. We spent twenty-five minutes talking about faith. He eventually declined my offer to go to Alpha, but I realized afterwards that God just wanted me to plant the seed. My project manager had never thought about the importance of faith and shared some private stories about his parents' faith and his upbringing with me. I can't assess the impact of the conversation: I simply hope that I planted some seeds that God will cultivate and grow. I never

would have had the opportunity if I would have just rejected that first thought that I should invite him to Alpha.

Identify your sphere of influence and commit to working in this space. Who is your flock? Jesus had three concentric circles in his ministry: the three (Andrew, James, and John), who were granted privileged access to him and insight into his mission; the twelve disciples, the company he selected and patiently trained; and the seventy-two (Luke 10:1–12), whom he sent out before him to the places he intended to visit. It is healthy and justified to have concentric rings of intimacy in your life—just do not let these rings of intimacy become rings of possessiveness! Which people in your life belong to the three, the twelve, and the seventy-two? How are you invited to be a different kind of influence in each successive ring?

Be Salt and Light: Discern between Presence and Distance

Balancing between presence and distance is the great interpersonal spiritual challenge of evangelization. Avoid the two extremes: chameleon Christianity, in which you do not bother to express the Christian distinctives through your way of life, and "Jacuzzi Christianity,"[21] wherein you separate entirely from non-Christians, preferring the gentler company of Christians to the complexities and tensions that involvement in the wider world entails. In the chameleon mode, it is often fear of disapproval that keeps us from wearing our true colors. While stuck in jacuzzi mode, we suffer from a different kind of deficit of courage: an aversion to risk, discomfort, and the unpredictability of relationships outside of our comfort zone—a reluctance to face the chill outside of the warm waters.

The Epistle to Diognetus, composed in the second century, marvelously captures the essence of the authentic Christian attitude, characterizing the Christian as a person who lives as an alien in their homeland, who participates in everything like a citizen but bears with everything like a pilgrim; one for whom every foreign land is a homeland and every homeland a foreign land.[22] The challenge of Christian life is to refrain from choosing exclusively in favor of either presence or distance in order to prematurely resolve the tension. Christians travel the earth as dual citizens, remaining committed to the good of the world as we set our

21. See FOCUS, "Incarnational Evangelization."
22. Diogn. 5.

sights on heaven. The maintenance of this attitude is not a trick, a posture, or an intellectual riddle, but rather the essence of Christian discipleship, reflecting the commitment to hold the tension of the love of God for the world with the reality of the world's neglect of God. This is nothing less than the paschal dynamic, the tension Jesus laid upon himself and carried to the cross! Consequently, as we grapple with discerning our place, we must not expect to experience only smoothness and ease, but rather something of the weight of Christ's cross.

Be a Disciple-Maker: Invest in Small Groups and in Particular People

We must make God's vision our own, seeing each person as possessed of an infinite value. It is important to invest in and spend time with people, even when we feel that we are pulled away from tasks that rightfully occupy us. Pope Francis often repeats that he likes to ask parents whether they waste time with their children, whether they take time out from work to play with their kids. He encourages parents to do so more often. Clearly, on his own estimation, this "wasted time" is the more valuable use of time. Likewise, to spend time with others in our community is not a waste. Our dedication to others will bear fruit, but incrementally, until the day comes when we appreciate how all the small decisions to temporarily place our projects aside have contributed to the light and togetherness of our community.

In the book of Acts, Jesus tells his apostles that the Holy Spirit will come upon them, and they will be his witnesses in Jerusalem, Judea, and Samaria, and to the end of the world (Acts 1:8). No surprise that the end of the world falls at the end of his list of places; when we start a ministry, we must begin with Jerusalem. First form a small group and start to grow with them. Remember that the few, rather than the many—in Newman's words, "the resolute, undaunted, zealous few"—change society. In an era in which it may be difficult to envision the large-scale transformation of culture, we must recall the personal influence paradox: large-scale transformation is not driven by large-scale efforts.

Do not be afraid to ask for radicality of commitment: it is not necessarily better to be greater in numbers. Throughout the Old Testament, we see the development of the notion of the remnant, the small group that maintains faithfulness in the midst of religious and social crisis and the general abdication of the people of Israel. This is the group that transmits the faith to the next generation, keeping the candle burning, as it were, up until the time of Christ. The remnant concept resonates in a period in which the Church in the West has suffered a steady decline in numbers. In fact, Pope Benedict XVI foresaw the predicament. In a radio address he gave in 1970 as Cardinal Joseph Ratzinger, asked about the face of the Church in the year 2000, he said:

> In the crisis of today, the Church of tomorrow will emerge—a Church that has lost much. She will become small and will have to start afresh more or less from the beginning. She will no longer be able to inhabit many of the edifices she built in prosperity. As the number of her adherents diminishes, so will she lose many of her social privileges. . . . The Church will be a more spiritual Church. . . . She may well no longer be the dominant social power to the extent she was until recently; but she will enjoy a fresh blossoming and be seen as man's home, where he will find life and hope beyond death.[23]

Clearly, Cardinal Ratzinger's diagnosis goes beyond lament, even expressing optimism about the deep-seated strength of this slimmed Church. We may share in his judgment: if the Church is to be smaller, then it is also to be more densely packed with holiness. For the flourishing of a smaller, denser Church, we must seek to build groups made up of the zealous few—zealous in their radical love of Christ, but zealous too in their determination to go into the world and invest in relationships within the Church and without. In our intrepid work of evangelization, varied as it may be, personal influence is to be the permeating factor and integrating force of the whole of our activity.

---

23. Ratzinger, "Church Will Become Small."

CHAPTER NINE

Proclamation: Worldview and Christian Worldview

WHAT IS THE DIFFERENCE in worldview that gives rise to differences in values? What is the fundamental framework of vision, of belief, and of meaning, perhaps not fully conscious, that guides one person to see life in one way and another to take up a divergent position?

In the course of evangelization, we find evident disparities—sometimes vast—between the core tenets of the worldview of those coming to faith and those more established in a life of discipleship. Significantly, however, these disparities do not constitute an unbridgeable gap. Once a person awakens to Christ, a reconciling force intervenes, drawing the new believer into closer union with their brothers and sisters in Christ; the dynamism of the Holy Spirit—a dynamism often resisted but never absent—draws them towards the more complete assimilation and integration of the Christian worldview.

To present this worldview and to lead others towards deepened appreciation and grasp of it—this is the great, crowning task of evangelization. But so that we are not daunted by the weight of our task, let us remember the reasons we have to be confident about our fitness. God assists us in making the Christian worldview our own, igniting our natural desire for knowledge and elevating this desire to a new plane by the light of the Spirit. God wants us to know him and his plan for humankind, incomparably more than say our most inspired literature teacher wanted us to know Homer. He will lead us to knowledge of him. Also, lest we think we are all called to ceaseless mental labor, we should bear in mind that integrating the Catholic-Christian worldview is not chiefly about amassing information: it is a process that must take place on the level of the soul if it is to sink into the mind. In T. S. Eliot's 1934 poem "Choruses from the Rock," the speaker asks, "Where is the wisdom we have lost in knowledge? Where is the knowledge we have lost in information?"[1] How true is this cry in our current cultural moment! The assimilation of the Christian worldview reverses the habituated priorities of our age, placing wisdom above its shriveled substitutes. Truly, it is not through frantic consumption, but rather through the steady practice of putting on the mind of Christ that we make the Christian worldview our own.

∾ ∾ ∾

Suppose you are taking a friend to view a championship match for a sport they have never seen before or, alternatively, that you are bringing a friend to the gallery of an exceptional painter whose artistic context is unfamiliar to them. Especially if you are an enthusiast, on the way over you would explain the rules, the history, and particular excitement of the game, or the genre, the cultural background, personal history, and special gifts of the painter. You would seek to shape your friend's mind to be prepared to receive the fresh experience with understanding. In our present culture, in which many people operate on a cultural and mental plane a great distance away from Christian belief, this is a taste of the task at hand: we are enthusiasts of an often unknown greatness.

The dissemination of the Christian worldview is the accompaniment that the proclamation of the kerygma ultimately demands. The kerygma requires backup: it must be contextualized and reinforced. The Christian worldview, or the Christian vision, is the right soil for the seed of the kerygma to sprout. In the era of Christendom, this "plant," so to speak, was native. The soil of Christendom was richer in supporting the flourishing of the Christian imagination. Through magnificent architecture (the city or town centered around the church or cathedral), political overlap (the recognition and promotion of the Christian religion in the public sphere), and popular language and sensibility (Christian symbols and motifs dominant in culture), the public mind led to and encouraged the personal absorption and comprehension of the kerygma.[2]

Now, with Christianity no longer at the forefront of our culture, we encounter a different situation. Whereas Christianity stood as the ruling

1. "Choruses from the Rock," in Eliot, *Rock*.
2. Cf. Shea, *From Christendom*, 20–22.

vision during the Christendom phase, in the West today, the majority abide by a non-Christian vision. We have entered another apostolic period, wherein Christians must introduce Jesus Christ to the unfamiliar and uninformed.[3] It would be incorrect to say that one particular worldview has gained ascendancy to take the place of Christianity, or even that a collection of clearly demarcated worldviews has risen to the surface; rather, a shifting and shuffling set of worldviews, partly overlapping, partly incompatible—an unstable synthesis of world religions, scientific materialism, hedonistic consumerism, neo-existentialism, and New Age spirituality and psychology—has combined to form what we might label the modern "marketplace of worldviews."

We need to bear in mind that this range of competing worldviews influences people who hear the kerygma. Previous interests and commitments present obstacles, even as seeds of the Word generate curiosity. Contrasting worldviews may need to be purified—or abandoned outright—as people move along a path of discipleship. Even when it comes to Catholics in the pews, we cannot suppose that the Christian vision has taken deep root. Just as much for Catholics as for newcomers, we must be ready to give an explanation for our hope (1 Pet 3:15).

This explanation begins with the joy of the gospel. Preaching the moral vision of Christianity at the outset tends to be premature. As the moral teachings of the faith emanate from and are rightfully situated within the broader imaginative vision, non-Christians who are instructed about morality off the bat will typically struggle to swallow the moral teachings. Seeing as they bring their assumptions and preconceptions (rather than the Christian worldview) to meet these teachings, they are prone to shallow and distorted interpretations. Such initial difficulty may then become a barrier to further exploration. Just as to get to know a person's values you must first get a sense of their worldview, the best and most responsible way to inform others about the content of our faith is to share the Christian vision. We can certainly be inventive and share according to new approaches, helping people to grasp the worldview little by little. But first and foremost, we have to believe—and be truly convinced of the beauty that we strive to transmit. This is what makes intellectual conversion compelling.

We call the process of intellectual conversion "evangelization of the mind," or *metanoia*. The Greek word *metanoia* means quite literally to change (*meta*) the mind (*noia/nous*). We are sometimes predisposed to

3. Shea, *From Christendom*, 29–30.

think of conversion in terms of change in lifestyle. This is part of the picture, but there can be no change in lifestyle without a change of mentality—no behavior change without the adoption of a new set of coordinates set down upon a new map of reality. As we examine the foundational structures and indicators of intellectual conversion, we aim to give a preliminary sketch of this map. We begin by identifying the core tenets of any worldview, Christian or otherwise. Then, we look specifically at the Christian worldview, examining some of the primary elements that distinguish the Christian outlook from alternative perspectives. Lastly, we mark the path to gaining a Christian worldview.

Defining Worldview

James H. Olthius gives an excellent introductory definition of worldview in his essay "On Worldviews" in the book *Stained Glass: Worldviews and Social Science*:

> A worldview is an intellectual framework or set of fundamental beliefs through which we view and judge the world. This vision need not be fully articulated: it may be so internalized that it goes largely unquestioned. . . . This vision is a channel for the ultimate beliefs which give direction and meaning to life. It is the integrative and interpretative framework by which order and disorder are judged; it is the standard by which reality is managed and pursued.[4]

Using Olthius's definition as a foundation, let's examine the principal features that apply for each person's worldview. Each worldview:

- Provides an internalized vision of reality.
- Grounds itself on first principles.
- May be partially unconscious or not fully articulated.
- Flows forth from multiple sources.
- Shapes both perception and behavior.
- May be true or false.
- Can be expressed in the form of a narrative that provides a sense of meaning.

---

4. As quoted in Sire, *Universe Next Door*, 18.

A Worldview Provides an Internalized Vision of Reality

A worldview creates a lens or filter through which we see reality. The Enlightenment ambition to perceive reality free from conditioning and established modes of interpretation—and thus to be possessed of a kind of pure, unclouded, unmediated objectivity and insight—has proven to be a naïve assumption. The construction of meaning and the habit of interpretation are so inherent to the human being that to aim for a kind of skeptical distance from all worldviews is intellectually tantamount to seeking to operate more efficiently by screening out the "bias" of one of the five senses. Worldviews can be true or false, and it is our obligation as thinking people to assess them critically and distinguish between them. However, this necessary sifting cannot mean ridding ourselves entirely of mediating symbols and frameworks, Christian or otherwise: to sweep the house clean of one worldview does not mean the house will remain clean—and may bring seven new paradigms in its place. We will invariably find ourselves taking up a certain holistic vision of the world or juggling several.

Philosopher James Sire delineates ten foundational worldviews—including Christian theism, deism, naturalism, and existentialism—but no list is apt to be exhaustive. Moreover, clear-cut distinctions fail to capture the jumbled way that worldviews reside in our minds. You will never meet a "pure existentialist," for instance; existentialism will invariably be accompanied by a medley of other perspectives to bulwark the vision of freedom and self-determination that inspires the existential thinker. Worldviews do tend to compete for dominance, however. They do seek, by their own intrinsic vigor, to push one another out, like wild animals jostling for control. But the dominant view does not necessarily succeed in completely eradicating the others; often, the weaker animals survive, carving out a dark corner of the woods and occasionally dashing through the clearing. Our own experience confirms this complex, fluid picture: zones of cognitive dissonance remain a feature of each of our mental lives. In any case, several basic questions can serve to identify what resides within:

1. What is the nature of external reality—that is, the world around us?

2. What is the nature of the fundamental reality, the "really real"?

3. What happens to us when we die?

4. What is a human person?

5. How do we determine what is right and wrong?

A Worldview Grounds Itself on First Principles

ᴊᴏʜɴ Henry Newman elucidated the pivotal and insufficiently recognized influence of what he called "first principles" on the whole of a person's mind. He considered first principles to be the invisible standards by which each person judges reality, the separating factors between proponents of different religions, the great determinants of our allegiances, and the final word regarding our personal characters. He defines first principles as follows:

> There are opinions and beliefs which do not depend on previous grounds, which are not drawn from facts for which no reasons can be given, or no sufficient reasons, which proceed immediately from the mind, and which the holder considers to be, as it were, part of himself.
>
> They are the means of proof, and are not themselves proved; they rule and are not ruled; they are sovereign on the one hand, irresponsible on the other: they are absolute monarchs, and if they are true, they act like the best and wisest of fathers to us: but, if they are false, they are the most cruel and baneful of tyrants. Yet, from the nature of our being, there they are, as I have said; there they must ever be. They are our guides and standards in speculating, reasoning, judging, deliberating, deciding, and acting; they are to the mind what the circulation of the blood and the various functions of our animal organs are to the body. They are the conditions of our mental life; by them we form our view of events, of deeds, of persons, of lines of conduct, of aims, of moral qualities, of religions. They constitute the difference between man and man; they characterize him. As determined by his First Principles, such is his religion, his creed, his worship, his political party, his character, except as far as adventitious circumstances interfere with their due and accurate development; they are, in short, the man.[5]

As such, first principles are the building blocks of worldviews: to know a set of first principles is to be on your way to understanding a worldview, in the same way that a sketch indicates the shape of a finished painting.

Implicit in a Christian understanding of worldview is the basic movement of conversion: we convert *from* holding, inconsistent, unpurified, or untruthful first principles *into* the fullness of the Christian worldview, a worldview grounded in first principles that flow forth from Christ himself and the great story of salvation that he fully reveals to us. Our first principles usually go unexamined: they are the presuppositions at

5. AP, pt. 3.

the foundation of our everyday reasoning and analysis. Though often held unreflectively, they are so pivotal as to essentially establish the character of a person, as John Henry Newman argues.

Whether we are engaging in introspection or considering others who stand at a certain stage of conversion, we will find the same thing occurring: Christ is inviting us to either purify or drop certain guiding first principles that shape our lives and commitments—leading us to complete a partially formed principle with the fullness of his model or to replace alien principles with those coordinated with his mind. We *transcend and include*, or we *jettison and substitute*. Ultimately, Christ invites us not only to grasp the Christian worldview more fully but also to conform our actions to it. We are acting as his disciples when we transform our theory into practice. Those who have achieved this task with a special intensity and comprehensiveness are the saints.

Given that our first principles tend to be held unconsciously, the effort to conform our actions to the Christian worldview requires a degree of subtleness of skill, openness to new insight, and dedication to discovery. We are to be like psychoanalysts, uncovering the springs that lie behind the thoughts and orientations to which we are habituated. Although the task presents a challenge, it also offers a great reward: the capacity to see the world in a fresh light, and the chance to develop a deepened picture of reality capable of recognizing core motivations and strivings. To help another (or to help yourself) perceive first principles can be a vital move in the conversion journey that pushes the boat off the rocks and enables it to continue floating downstream. This maneuver is all the more effective when we can compare and contrast a certain principle with the Christian vision, the clear pool into which the river empties.

Do not be surprised if, in addressing a particular first principle, a whole constellation of thought follows. First principles grip our minds, reinforce themselves, lead to concrete actions, and shape our personalities. Organically, they either confirm and support additional principles and perspectives, or oppose and expel them. If we evaluate how they influence the mind, will, and sentiments, then perhaps first principles are the guards of our castle, allowing in some thoughts while turning back others. They must be not only that but also the counselors of the king's court—carrying priority messages, weighing the meaning and significance of events, and pointing to courses of action. They might be the horses that pull the carriages of our wills to a particular destination. They are the seeds that first take root and later flower across the garden of our tastes and preferences, shaping us to marvel at some things and not others. In short, first principles are the primary material of our thought processes—and, in the end, no less than the stuff of our destiny.

A Worldview May Be Only Partially Conscious

Our societies mediate worldviews subtly and cumulatively, as media, traditions, storytelling, implicit forms of communication, and received wisdom combine to form a prevailing outlook. Most people simply reflect what they have received. To uncover your worldview requires stepping out from your ordinary frame of reference in order to glimpse this frame as if from a remote vantage point: it is an inherently philosophical operation, and never quite achieved to completion, for we cannot step totally outside of our own point of view. A worldview is not something we see, not an object of our experience, but rather *that through which we see* everything else; this feature constitutes both its power and its elusiveness.

A Worldview Flows from Multiple Sources

When we assess particular worldviews, we can trace genealogies, or family trees, of ideas. We can follow these long lines of descent through scientific, philosophical, and religious texts, but even these texts can be interpreted further (and themselves informed) through cultural matrices and the idiosyncratic tempers of peoples. Texts do not tell the whole story: to understand living ideas—ideas that take root in *living* people—we must appeal to a living history. To recapitulate this history, we must encompass facts of religion, philosophy, education, geography, culture, politics, and personal experience, both traumatic and positive. We must give heed to all of these sources of influence. And then we would still have to leave space for free will, the factor that necessarily remains beyond rational investigation or elucidation. Explaining why a person embraces their chosen worldview involves honoring multiple complex sources that we can begin to grasp—and one complex source that we cannot: the mystery of the human will.

A Worldview Shapes Both Our Perception and Our Behavior

It is not an overstatement to say that worldviews inspire, facilitate, reinforce, interpret, and guide all of our actions. Since worldviews are the intellectual framework through which we receive new information, our foundational worldview shapes our appreciation of and reaction to things, people, and events. Not only that, but worldviews are recursive: whenever we interpret new information, we feed that information back into our default worldview, thus strengthening the entire system. Worldviews are not simply like lenses that color our reality with certain hues. We also must understand them as being like snowballs rolling downhill, picking up the material along their path, gaining mass as they travel.

To understand precisely why people behave the way they do, it is often necessary to stand inside their worldview. For instance, in Catholic spirituality, we witness actions that are confounding by nearly every outside standard. Why would someone leave their home and sell all of their possessions in order to become a monk? Why do believers embark upon a course of fasting and penance during the season of Lent? Why do priests take a vow of celibacy? Why do Catholics receive the Eucharist with such solemnity? These are a few of the questions that are effectively grasped only by seeing with the eyes of a Christian.

A Worldview May Be True or False

Worldviews are not necessarily accurate or complete. As individuals and as collectives alike, we are prone to deceptions and untruths. We are capable of holding an erroneous idea for a long time. When we come to the truth out of falsehood, we experience something of a crisis. One of our priests in the Saint John Society, born in Spain and raised in Argentina, grew up convinced that the Grand Canyon was located in California. He was skeptical when, hearing the proposed route for his society's road trip across the United States, a fellow priest mentioned they would stop off at the Grand Canyon on their way through Arizona. He suppressed his confusion at the moment. But then he was shocked as he got out of the car to look around *in Arizona*, and his brother priest pointed to show him the Grand Canyon stretching out before him! He did not want to believe his eyes: the thing he had taken for fact his whole life was proven in an instant to be inaccurate. Actually, he was somewhat shaken! Granted this is a simplistic example;

untruths that we live with affect our lives and actions to varying degrees. So too, groups and societies are capable of enduring in error. Think of the view of the Catholic Church and that of strict scientific materialists: one group must be right, and one must be wrong.

Saint Augustine, on his way into the Catholic Church, experienced the crumbling of a series of worldviews, each in turn put to the test by his freshly acquired knowledge and experience. Not only did he find letting go of his previously held perspectives difficult, but he also grew angry at the people who had kept him captivated by false ideas. For Augustine, the deception as to the nature of ultimate truth was the most egregious deception of all. The worldview that detained him for the longest period was that of the Manichaeans, a heretical, dualistic sect that wildly reinterpreted the Christian Scriptures, believing that they possessed an alternative, esoteric knowledge of reality, accessible only to their privileged group. For nine years as a young man, Augustine was a Manichaean adherent. As he writes in his *Confessions*, reflecting upon the period, the Manichaeans persistently disappointed him but continued to keep him committed: "All they set before me were dishes of glittering myths. . . . Yet I ate those offerings, believing I was feeding on [God]."[6] He deems himself to have been vulnerable to the "subtle maneuverings"[7] of the Manichaeans not because he was careless about the truth but because he desired it so ardently. Their counterfeit version of the truth hooked him by virtue of the attraction of the genuine artifact. He writes ruefully, "I supposed that I was approaching the truth when in fact I was moving away from it."[8]

Augustine's nine-year wandering is not altogether uncommon. It is difficult and painful to break away from a dominant paradigm that you have dedicated yourself to for a long time, even when the paradigm is unfruitful. By virtue of being attached to a certain group, by being surrounded by those who profess the group's philosophy, you can struggle to gain insight into the falsehood, errors, or half-truths that may plague the association. More subtly, falsehood often imitates the truth or elevates a partial, distorted aspect of it. Consequently, you may, like Augustine, continue for a time supposing that you are approaching the truth, when in fact you are being moved in the opposite direction. Once you have broken out of the inadequate framework and into a new vision, you come to face the further anxiety of being

6. Augustine, *Conf.* 3.6.10.

7. Augustine, *Conf.* 3.7.12.

8. Augustine, *Conf.* 3.7.12.

bereft of a stable outlook on the world. On this shifting sand, judgments and decisions become more complex and more dubious. You occupy a liminal or in-between space: You no longer stand squarely in the territory of the old worldview, but you have not yet come to occupy a different sphere. The interpersonal challenge also intervenes, for as you no longer authentically belong to the community that shared this core perspective, you grow progressively to feel like an alien in a place that used to be a home for you. This dynamic is destabilizing for any human being: the collapse of a worldview always includes, to a certain degree, an existential collapse as well. But it is no tragedy; the dissolution of the previous way of seeing represents a positive moment, even if negatively perceived. It is a triumph of the truth and righteousness over illusion and convenience in your life. By clearing out the former view, you create space to come to know and live the truth, to step into a more abundant, more honest, and more fulfilling life. Ascertained from this perspective, the challenge and promise of passing through the thresholds of conversion become all the more evident.

A Worldview Takes on a Narrative Form

A new worldview means a new story—a new way of situating yourself, other people, your culture, and human history. Our stories are the nourishment of the soul. The stories we tell, the "master narratives" of mythology, philosophy, and religion, provide the meaning that our souls need to stay alive, engaged, and hopeful. Joseph Chilton Pearce (1926–2016) devised the image of the "Cosmic Egg of Meaning" to help us understand this life-giving, perspective-shaping function of narratives. The core idea is that we live in a nested set (egg) of stories—stretching from the personal to the communal to the universal—and we experience fulfillment and meaning when these levels are well coordinated among each other. When we have an experience of this harmony, when we perceive that "it is all one egg," we relate to a meaningful universe.

We can view the inner part of the egg, the yolk, as our own personal story, *my story*: our personal development, our education, our subjective point of view, our traumas and our triumphs. At the next level, in the white of the egg, we have *our story*: the groups to which we belong, including family, nation, and other loyalties, all of which nourish and supply a protected space for the yolk—our personal story. "Our story" expands our sense of self, bringing us into relationship with others. Then, at the outermost layer, the great shell that encloses both particular groups and our small selves, we have *the story*, the ultimate reality that gives form to the whole. At this level, we are connected to the ground of being itself and to the realm of transcendent truth.

Great and true stories range across all these levels in a way that knits them together, honoring both microcosm and macrocosm, our place in the cosmos and the cosmos entire. In the biblical tradition, we witness the coexistence and interpenetration of the three levels. Christ, as Paul puts it, gave his life for *me* (Gal 2:20)! And yet, as Paul speaks of this single "me," he understands that the "me" saved by Christ is inducted into the whole history of the people of Israel, grafted onto their story. Moreover, God's plan for Israel opens onto all of humanity and creation: Israel is an instrument for the salvation of the whole world. Christ himself, the Messiah of Israel, is the *Logos*, the meaning and pattern of all of creation. In a Christian worldview then, we have an exemplary case of this Cosmic Egg of Meaning, whether we proceed from the individual to the universal or vice versa: in telling *the* story, we must appeal to *our* story, both of which ultimately ground the redemption of *my* story.

The Christian Worldview:
The Stages of Salvation

To be fully converted to Christ means to have acquired a new worldview. The Christian worldview entails the unity of the Cosmic Egg of Meaning—the unity of universal, particular, and personal: the one who receives this story of salvation moves from spectator to participant, finding themselves directly addressed. As we have discussed, this is precisely what is unique about the kerygma: it implicates both storyteller and listener; it calls you into the central action of the great story of Jesus. As we grow in faith, as we live out the story of salvation in our own personal, unrepeatable manner, we grow in our sensitivity to the distinctive Christian worldview.

To develop the Christian worldview to a satisfying degree exceeds the scope of this book. However, we can convey some core features that belong intrinsically to the great story of salvation. The best place to begin is the first paragraph of the catechism, which summarizes this story as follows:

> God, infinitely perfect and blessed in himself, in a plan of sheer goodness freely created man to make him share in his own blessed life. For this reason, at every time and every place, God

draws close to man. He calls man to seek him, to know him, to love him with all his strength. He calls together all men, scattered and divided by sin, into the unity of his family, the Church. To accomplish this, when the fullness of time had come, God sent his Son as Redeemer and Savior. In his Son and through Him, he invites men to become, in the Holy Spirit, his adopted children and thus heirs of his blessed life.[9]

In the next paragraphs, the catechism states that in response we are to evangelize, like the apostles sharing Christ, "so that this call should resound throughout the world."[10] When we carry the light of faith onwards and outwards, we are carrying forth this vision. The core elements translate into the attitude evinced by converted Christians: because we trust in the final victory, we remain free from despair; because of the inherent value of each human being, we respect all whom we encounter; because we know that we are pilgrims and that God is our treasure, we exercise detachment from material things; and because we try to transform this world in sight of Christ's coming kingdom, we work for progress. We land on optimism because we trust in a love—"the love that moves the sun and the stars"[11]—that makes new, redeems, and fulfills. We stay open to awe because we believe that all of reality is a sacrament of God's presence, that visible reality manifests elements of the invisible world. And we learn humility before a God who reveals himself to us, showing us a meaning *given to us* rather than *created by us.*

This revelation of God, sketched in the previous catechism paragraph, also reveals the heart of the Christian worldview. Revelation is no less than God's self-communication, offered to us in a way that we can understand. The whole design is the design of *salvation history.* We can separate five big moments or stages that are indispensable to our understanding of this story of salvation—a pocket guide, if you will, to the stages of salvation history.

1. **Creation:** God, an eternal communion of love, created this world to share his love with us. We therefore see reality as emanating from the mind and the heart of God—a mind and heart not governed by necessity, but rather motivated by love in freedom. The world is a visible manifestation of God, reflecting the goodness, truth, and beauty inherent to God. We see this world as a rich, supersaturated cosmos—as

9. CCC, §1.

10. CCC, §2.

11. Quote from author Ceragioli's memory of Dante, *Paradiso,* canto 27.

a place that is lovely, full of truth, and an icon of the beauty of God. In this world, the human person is a steward or representative of the king who is sovereign over it.

2. **Fall:** The original order and beauty was damaged by the influence of an evil principle—precisely, by our complicity in the wicked intentions of a being set against God. Sin introduces suspicion towards God, disruption among human beings (tending towards violence), and division within the human person. Awareness of this triple disharmony is a part of our Christian worldview, which even as it retains an optimism that overcomes doubt and despair, recognizes the evil present in our world and in ourselves. Healing and redemption lead to communion—the reintegration of what has grown divided due to sin—while sin and brokenness pull us apart and contribute to fragmentation.

3. **Redemption:** God did something about the sinful, disordered, and disoriented state of humanity. As Saint Athanasius surmises in his fourth-century *On the Incarnation*, God could not stand to see his creatures in such a pitiful condition, and driven by an overwhelming spirit of compassion, chose to act by sending his beloved Son to remedy our plight. In the medieval period, Saint Thomas Aquinas formalized the explanation for the incarnation with these four reasons: God sent his Son in order to forgive us, to provide us an example to live by, to show us the depth of his love for us, and to sanctify us (that is, to enable us to become more like God). Jesus came to restore original order and beauty—and to make out of us a new creation in God. His coming, announced by the prophets, signaled the fullness of time. The incarnation is the high point of salvation history—the marriage of heaven and earth. Through Jesus's death on the cross—a death in which he carried his incarnation to its final goal—New Life was made available to us. The fruits of Jesus's redemption are the outpouring of "grace upon grace" proclaimed in the Gospel of John (John 1:16). We are forgiven. We are sanctified by the Holy Spirit. We become children of the Father in Jesus. We become a part of Christ's spiritual body and brothers and sisters in Christ. We become heirs to his kingdom and recipients of eternal life.

4. **Sanctification:** Through the action of the Church, these fruits of Christ's redemption flow down to people across all subsequent ages. The seven

sacraments provide a channel of God's grace, making the salvation of Christ available to each individual. This process of incorporating the fruits of Christ's redemption—of living according to the intentions of his redeeming sacrifice—we name sanctification.

5. **Glorification:** The plan that Jesus enacted is like a seed maturing towards full growth. Through his incarnation, he inaugurated a new era. We live simultaneously in the "already" of this era and the "not yet" of final fulfillment at the end of time. We trust in the promises Jesus has made regarding that time: He will come in glory through a second public, victorious, and definitive coming. He will judge the living and the dead. He will transform the world we know into a new creation, bringing forth a new heaven and a new earth unimaginable in their splendor. He will raise us up, and sickness and death will be defeated. We are asked to place our total confidence in these prophecies. As we read in Ephesians: "May the eyes of [your] hearts be enlightened, that you may know what is the hope that belongs to his call, what are the riches of glory in his inheritance among the holy ones" (Eph 1:18).

Developing a Christian Worldview

We live in a time in which we cannot doubt that the process of "conversion" makes manifest the full meaning of the word; it is a time when conversion means to turn around, to change, not only in one's inner spirit but also in the vision absorbed through education received both formally and informally. It is a time when becoming authentically Christian means to go against the grain and resist dominant, entrenched perspectives and notions. The holistic Christian vision is the fruit of this holistic conversion: the mind comes alive in Christ through the reexamination of first principles, the trusting surrender to the standards of sacred Scripture, the acceptance and personal integration of the story of salvation, and the correlation of the big picture of discipleship with the moral and spiritual practices of the Church.

We must be patient however, with ourselves and with others, as conversion unfolds. Conversion is a slow process, and sometimes susceptible to stalls, even to apparent backwards motion, as we become more acutely aware of our sinfulness, pride, and interior resistances. The intellectual component in particular demands not only the reformation of desire and of habit but also the time and effort needed to accustom ourselves to a new way of thinking and perceiving. For example, how do we transition from a vision of the events of our lives as disconnected, haphazard, and random to a vision centered upon God's providence? We must first accept providence as a theological truth. We must accept that God constantly shapes and guides our lives for our good and in the direction of our salvation. We can deepen our trust in God's providence through meditation and prayer—perhaps recollecting the wisdom displayed in the ordering of our destiny throughout the stages of our life, or praying with Jesus's reassuring declaration that God knows even the number of hairs on our heads (Matt 10:30). But then comes the difficult part: When we are met with the unforeseen event, the frustrating setback, the apparent misfortune, how do we digest these moments while remaining faithful to the providential vision? Do we complain about the blows of "blind fate," as we perhaps felt entitled to do in the past, or do we find a way to read the challenging dimensions of our lives in the light of God's providence?

In this final question lies the crucial difference between knowledge of the Christian worldview and integration of the Christian worldview. An increase of the former without the latter makes one something more of a scholar but not necessarily more of a Christian; the Christian brain must sit at the feet of the Christian mind. In the end, attainment of the greater goal depends upon trust in Jesus. We cannot adequately receive the teachings of Jesus if we are not his disciples. Our trust feeds a virtuous cycle: the more we trust and believe in him, the more we listen to him. The more we listen, the more we think like him, and the more we think like him, the more we understand! Communion of heart requires communion of mind, and vice versa. As the great theologians remind us, "You must believe in order to understand" (cf. Isa 7:9). Initial, or better put, *initiating* belief starts off the great, ever-intensifying quest that spurs on both understanding of the Christian mysteries and faith in them. The first step—the step neither simpleton nor sage can skip—is to become a disciple through making an act of faith; only then does the Christian worldview begin to settle into place. The action of the Holy Spirit leads us onward, while the assimilation of the Christian vision remains a task that requires our effort like any other worthwhile endeavor.

Gaining a Christian worldview includes two movements: purification and renewal. Saint Paul says in the Letter to the Romans, "Do not conform yourselves to this age but be transformed by the renewal of your mind, that you may discern what is the will of God, what is good and pleasing and perfect" (Rom 12:1–2). We may justly interpret conformity "to this age" as adherence, conscious or unconscious, to false principles, ideologies, and doubts that shape our thinking. Part of our task becomes to discover the source and impact of these principles so as to place aside all that is contrary to the gospel. This is the first half of Saint Paul's exhortation: the task of purification.

Following Romans, such purification is a necessary step on the way to part two of the exhortation: the renewal of the mind. Purification creates the potential for renewal. To be "transformed by the renewal of your mind" is the goal of assimilation of the Christian worldview. To transform—literally, to *change the form*—means to change the fundamental pattern of your thinking. The new pattern is the pattern laid out by Jesus: to think as he thinks, to see reality from his point of view, to "put on the mind of Christ" (Phil 2:5). We can rely on the following means to develop this Christified mind, to receive the new form through which we grow to irradiate the light of faith:

- **Spiritual meditation:** The catechism expresses the power of Christian meditation: "Meditation engages thought, imagination, emotion, and desire. This mobilization of faculties is necessary in order to deepen our convictions of faith, prompt the conversion of our heart, and strengthen our will to follow Christ. Christian prayer tries above all to meditate on the mysteries of Christ, as in *lectio divina* or the rosary. This form of prayerful reflection is of great value, but Christian prayer should go further: to the knowledge of the love of the Lord Jesus, to union with him."[12] Through prayer with the word of God, we develop a personal sense for the convictions of our faith. Scripture is a great sacrament of Jesus's presence in the world: prayerful reading of Scripture puts us into contact with Jesus—precisely in the way that a sacrament mediates invisible spiritual reality. Prayer with the daily Gospel stabilizes this relationship with the Lord, keeping us open to his influence habitually rather than intermittently.

- **Study of our faith:** In addition to prayerful meditation, study of Scripture broadens our view of the story of salvation. We observe the evolution towards Christ in the Old Testament and the revelation of Christ in the New. We learn to see the pointed allusions and layers of

12. CCC, §2708.

meaning present in the familiar words of Jesus, adding a foundation, full of treasures and artifacts, to our understanding of the Gospels. Study of theology adds another dimension, synthesizing and thematizing the story of God's love found in the Scriptures and throughout Church tradition. As with theology, the writings of the saints activate the mind, but they also have a particular impact on the will, inspiring us to greater heights of sanctity and devotion. The saints' diversity of circumstances and personalities remind us of the variety of paths leading towards fulfillment in Christ: the saints broaden our imagination for what is possible for us!

- **Celebration of the liturgical year:** Closeness to the Eucharist brings our study of faith to the level of the tangible and the embodied. The unique gift of the Catholic liturgy is its combination of word and gesture. The parts of the Mass are culled from the Bible; the Mass is essentially constructed out of Scripture but such that Scripture may be *enacted*—so that we can bow before the Lord (Phil 2:10), humbly invite him under our roof (Matt 8:8), and partake of the bread of life (John 6:35). Our celebration of the Mass becomes all the more charged when we pay attention to and make our own the rhythm of the liturgical year. Each year, as we go through Advent, Christmas, Lent, Easter, and Pentecost, we are exposed to the same narratives. But as we pass through these seasons possessed of deeper configuration to Christian community and deeper lives of prayer, we continue to meet these stories with fresh vision. The Word is born in our souls at Christmas. We die to self during Lent. The resurrection cry "He is alive!" mounts within us at Easter. We learn the meaning of spiritual springtime at Pentecost. For people of faith, the cyclical patterns of the liturgy do not produce a repetitive circular spiritual motion: we are not monotonously running around the same track. Rather, our path becomes a spiral, as we rise to new heights of appreciation, seeing the mysteries from a vantage point at once more elevated and more direct.

- **Participation within a community:** Only in the context of Christian community can discipleship fully come into its own: when we are surrounded by the body of Christ, Christianity makes sense across the various levels of our understanding. We must remember that the letters of the New Testament were addressed to particular communities, that the Gospels were the fruit of communal witness, and that the shared eucharistic banquet stands as the continuous Christian gathering force across time and space. For our spiritual life to click, for our missionary reach to extend, for the inner self and outer action to unify, it is important to seek out regular participation within community life. Only in the context of community can we "breathe in" the atmosphere of the Christian realm—and take on the bold, cohesive, and faithful outlook proper to its citizens.

Conclusion

WE LIKE TO REPEAT Saint Junipero Serra's missionary motto, "Always forward!" or, in Serra's native Spanish tongue, *Siempre adelante!* The phrase retains the greatest vitality in Spanish, but all the same, the message resounds. *Siempre adelante, nunca atrás.* Always forward, never back. This simple saying expresses the heart of the missionary attitude: move forward, always forward. Continue doing good even when adverse circumstances make your actions appear futile.

We are accustomed to hearing some variation on the theme that the river of faith is drying up at present, that it does not cut such a wide, inexorable course through the land as it did in the past. However, we cannot let this perspective dictate. We must go back to the fount; the resurrected heart of Jesus is the wellspring of New Life that flows into the world through the action of the Church. This river of life has never ceased flowing—winding through every kind of obstacle presented by our mixed earthly terrain, carrying on still amidst all manner of interruptions and forgetfulness across the ages. This current has influenced untold billions, and its power is undiminished today. It has produced saints who bear witness to its life-giving waters, saints whose very existences stand as a sign of the fruitfulness of the wellspring of New Life.

Let the personal testimonies, the theological principles, and the dynamic processes we have explored guide our response. But more than that, let us allow Jesus to find us in our questioning moments. Knowing our frailty and doubts, he promises us: "I am with you always" (Matt 28:20). "The gates of hell will not prevail" (Matt 16:18): this too is a word for our weariness—*and* our wariness. What to make, though, of the evident, verifiable falling away that we have seen for ourselves? He tells us that this eventuality does not indicate a blind spot in God's vision: "Because of the increase of evildoing, the love of many will grow cold. But the one who perseveres to the end will be saved" (Matt 24:12–13). Here is how we are to meet the moment: in the fellowship of the warm-hearted, we rejoice. When we find ourselves out in a chill, we persevere. The Church will never stop announcing Christ. As the Church, *we* will never stop announcing Christ. The river will not run dry because it flows from the one who has promised protection until the end.

All this is not to say that we blithely look past the reality of our context. The Church is called to take stock of the signs of the times and let herself be led by the hand of the Spirit. Both factors point to the Church's embrace of mission. Fewer of those who belong to the Church are coming regularly, and more people are leaving outright. We are no longer in the era of Christendom but have entered another apostolic period. In this situation, the Spirit of Jesus responds by inspiring people to live out the Great Commission with a new freshness and a reinvigorated action. In our missionary work, we have seen the Spirit guide towards this horizon. The teachings of the last popes (Paul VI, John Paul II, Benedict XVI, and Francis) are also aligned with the guidance of the Spirit and the needs of the Church. They exhort us to adopt a missionary heart and mind, to become a Church out on mission.

This cultural shift starts with the inner conviction that our main task as a missionary Church is to make disciples. As the Church exists to evangelize, so we exist to lead people to experience Christ and the New Life that he offers. We exist to invite people to dive into this river of life that flows from the heart of Jesus. These waters heal, liberate, and transform us into Christ. Through the action of the Spirit, those who dive in become more like him.

People are no longer coming forward to the river of life to be "sacramentalized"; a certain "stationary object" strategy and vision of the Church has had its day. We need to go out. The first step is to announce the kerygma. We must proclaim, in the power of the Spirit, what God has done in Jesus for each of us and for all of us. This is lesson 1. It is like the small glass of water that awakens thirst for the living waters. This is the initial proclamation, and it is the word by which people become disciples.

We must build up a Church of intentional disciples. We must bring about a Church filled with people who have experienced the New Life in Christ. We need many who remain inside the waters, who experience Christ, and cannot help but to say: "Master, it's good to be here!" We need people who can sincerely proclaim that they were previously of one mindset and now stand as a new creation—and that what happened in between point *A* and point *B* is Jesus. We must be a Church earnest in our conviction that Christianity is good news! Only then we will be a missionary church through and through. The experience of New Life that follows the proclamation of the kerygma is the foundational element in the whole construction.

How to get there? We have explored pathways. We can develop entrance doors that either make it easy to come back or to enter the Church for the first time. Through offering a testimony of life, we can become luminous witnesses of the New Life that lies in Jesus. We can combine personal influence and the sacramental system (the stone and the rain alike). And we can attain these initiatives through the development of pastoral centers where disciples can invite others by saying, "come and see." Should we do these things, we will persuade minds and move hearts through experiences of truth, goodness, and beauty. At all times, we must remain open to the power of the Spirit who sends us signs and wonders to renew our own faith and awaken the curiosity of seekers.

Now, transcendent of each of these action items is the spiritual necessity of remaining engrafted to the vine in order to bear fruit (John 15). We must "be with him" so as to proclaim with power (Mark 3:16). We must stay in Jerusalem to be clothed with power from on high (Acts 1:4). Union with Jesus, the anointing of the Holy Spirit, and supernatural power are needed for this great task of becoming a more resolutely missionary Church. The abundance of New Life in Christ is the root of all initiative—and all persuasion—in the New Evangelization.

In the face of any manner of discouragement and division, let us also pray for the grace of perseverance, hope, and the spirit of victory! Saint Paul says: "Let us not grow tired of doing good, for in due time we shall reap our harvest, if we do not give up" (Gal 6:9). Do not give in to negativity or fall prey to exhaustion! Keep sowing, and one day you will see the fruits of your work.

Persevere because the world needs it. The consequences of pushing God away from culture, from shared life, and from the life of the family are tragic. In militating against the experience of God, in neglecting communion, we lose not only the sense of the divine and transcendence but, moreover, the sense of what is quintessentially human.

Persevere because God wants it. He suffers when we suffer. He insists on entering this world and renewing it continuously. He wants to bless abundantly the servants who help him with this task.

Persevere because it is possible. In the Saint John Society, we say, "It is possible to evangelize." As a Church, we possess the spiritual, sacramental, and human resources to live out the call of the Great Commission.

Always forward, never backward! Keep moving forward without losing hope. Keep rooting yourself in Christ, and you will bear fruit. Keep waiting for him, and he will come.

Bibliography

Augustine. *Confessions*. Translated by R. S. Pine-Coffin. Baltimore: Penguin, 1961.

Balthasar, Hans Urs von. *The Word Made Flesh*. Vol. 1 of *Explorations in Theology*. San Francisco: Ignatius, 2011.

Barron, Robert. "What Makes the Church Grow?" *Word on Fire* (blog), December 9, 2015. https://www.wordonfire.org/articles/barron/what-makes-the-church-grow/.

Benedict XVI, Pope. "General Audience." Vatican, September 3, 2008. https://www.vatican.va/content/benedict-xvi/en/audiences/2008/documents/hf_ben-xvi_aud_20080903.html.

———. "General Audience." Vatican, October 24, 2012. https://www.vatican.va/content/benedict-xvi/en/audiences/2012/documents/hf_ben-xvi_aud_20121024.html.

———. *Jesus of Nazareth: Holy Week*. San Francisco: Ignatius, 2011.

Buber, Martin. *Between Man and Man*. New York: Routledge, 2002.

Cantalamessa, Raniero. "1st Advent Sermon, 2011." EWTN, December 8, 2011. https://www.ewtn.com/catholicism/library/1st-advent-sermon-2011-1779.

———. "2nd Advent Sermon, 2011." EWTN, December 15, 2011. https://www.ewtn.com/catholicism/library/2nd-advent-sermon-2011-1780.

———. "3rd Advent Sermon, 2011." EWTN, December 16, 2011. https://www.ewtn.com/catholicism/library/3rd-advent-sermon-2011-1782.

———. "4th Advent Sermon, 2011." EWTN, December 23, 2011. https://www.ewtn.com/catholicism/library/4th-advent-sermon-2011-1783.

———. *The Holy Spirit in the Life of Jesus: The Mystery of Christ's Baptism*. Collegeville, MN: Liturgical, 1994.

Center for Applied Research in the Apostolate (CARA). "Frequently Requested Church Statistics." CARA, n.d. https://cara.georgetown.edu/faqs.

Eliot, T. S. *The Rock*. Boston: Houghton Mifflin Harcourt, 2014.

Eusebius. "The Writings of Irenæus against the Schismatics at Rome." From *Church History: Nicene and Post-Nicene Fathers, Second Series*, edited and translated by Philip Schaff and Henry Wace, vol. 1. Grand Rapids: Eerdmans, 1890. https://biblehub.com/library/pamphilius/church_history/chapter_xx_the_writings_of_irenaeus.htm.

Fellowship of Catholic University Students (FOCUS). "Incarnational Evangelization: The Art of Accompaniment." FOCUS, n.d. https://focusequip.org/incarnational-evangelization-the-art-of-accompaniment/.

Gregory Nazianzen. "Oration 43." From *Cyril of Jerusalem, Gregory Nazianzen: Nicene and Post-Nicene Fathers, Second Series,* edited by Philip Schaff and Henry Wace, translated by Charles Gordon Browne and James Edward Swallow, vol. 7. Buffalo, NY: Christian Literature, 1894. Revised and edited for New Advent by Kevin Knight. https://www.newadvent.org/fathers/310243.htm.

Jenkins, Dallas, dir. *The Chosen.* Season 1, episode 2, "Shabbat." Aired April 21, 2019, on VidAngel. https://watch.thechosen.tv/episode/season-1-episode-2-shabbat.

Keating, Thomas. *The Daily Reader for Contemplative Living.* New York: Continuum, 2009.

Komar, Emilio. *La Vitalidad Intelectual y la Lucha por la identidad.* Buenos Aires: Sabiduría Cristiana, 2021.

Kreeft, Peter. "The Greatest Confession of Failure in Church History." In *Catholics and Protestants: What Can We Learn from Each Other?,* 32–35. San Francisco: Ignatius, 2017.

Mallon, James. *Divine Renovation: Bringing Your Parish from Maintenance to Mission.* Toronto: Novalis, 2014.

Manzoni, Alessandro. *I promessi sposi: or, The Betrothed Lovers: A Milanese Story of the Seventeenth Century.* Translated by G. W. Featherstonhaugh. Washington, DC: Green, 1834.

Martin, Ralph. *The Fulfillment of All Desire: A Guidebook for the Journey to God Based on the Wisdom of the Saints.* Steubenville, OH: Emmaus Road, 2006.

Philippe, Jacques. *Thirsting for Prayer.* Translated by Helena Scott. New Rochelle, NY: Scepter, 2014.

Ratzinger, Joseph. "The Church Will Become Small." From *Faith and the Future.* San Francisco: Ignatius, 2009. https://www.catholiceducation.org/en/religion-and-philosophy/spiritual-life/the-church-will-become-small.html.

Saad, Lydia. "Catholics' Church Attendance Resumes Downward Slide." Gallup, April 9, 2018. https://news.gallup.com/poll/232226/church-attendance-among-catholics-resumes-downward-slide.aspx.

Shea, James. *From Christendom to Apostolic Mission: Pastoral Strategies for an Apostolic Age.* Bismarck, ND: University of Mary Press.

Sire, James W. *The Universe Next Door: A Basic Worldview Catalog.* 6th ed. Downers Grove, IL: InterVarsity, 2020.

Thuan, Francis Xavier Nguyen Van. *Testimony of Hope: The Spiritual Exercises of Pope John Paul II.* Boston: Pauline, 2000.

Van Den Bergh, Edward. "Cardinal Newman and the Oratory." EWTN, September 15, 2010. From *L'Osservatore Romano,* Weekly Edition in English. https://www.ewtn.com/catholicism/library/cardinal-newman-and-the-oratory-5697.

Weddell, Sherry. *Forming Intentional Disciples: The Path to Knowing and Following Jesus.* Huntington, IN: Our Sunday Visitor, 2012.

Made in the USA
Middletown, DE
26 September 2023